WHEN GOD DOESN'T MAKE SENSE

*"Every page of this book was
written with someone in mind.
It is the person for whom life has
spiraled out of control. If you
are that wounded individual
to whom I have been speaking,
I pray that God will use my efforts
to strengthen you and repair your
shattered faith. The Lord is very
near—and He cares! So do I."*

From the Acknowledgments
by Dr. James Dobson
President, Focus on the Family

WHEN GOD DOESN'T MAKE SENSE

DR. JAMES DOBSON

Tyndale House Publishers, Inc.
Wheaton, Illinois

Also available on audiocassette from Tyndale Living Audio.

First printing of Living Books edition November 2001.

Living Books is a registered trademark of Tyndale House Publishers, Inc.

ISBN 0-8423-7062-5

Printed in the United States of America

02   01
 5   4   3   2   1

This book is dedicated with great appreciation
to Dr. R. T. Kendall, senior pastor at
Westminster Chapel, London. His insight
and suggestions were of invaluable assistance
in preparing the final manuscript. I am honored
to call this good man my friend.

Contents

Acknowledgments

So many people were helpful to me in the writing process. My deeply loved friends Ed and Elsa Prince provided a beautiful hideaway on Lake Michigan, where I spent long, uninterrupted hours in study. My secretary, Karen Bethany, chased a million details and kept the total project on target. Two trusted colleagues at Focus on the Family, Rev. H. B. London and Dr. Kenneth Ogden, read the initial draft and made invaluable suggestions. I am thankful, too, for Drs. R. C. Sproul and J. I. Packer, noted theologians and authors, taking time from their busy schedules to read and critique my manuscript. This is no small favor, since both of these gifted men receive hundreds of unsolicited manuscripts from writers and would-be authors each year.

I should also thank Rev. Reuben Welch, who preached a sermon nearly 20 years ago entitled, "When God Contradicts God." It started me thinking about the problem of unanswered questions and led eventually to the writing of this book. And how could I forget to acknowledge John Keller, who taught me how to use a Macintosh laptop computer? Neither of us thought this old dog could learn a new trick, but it happened—more or less. This kind and patient tutor received several dozen frantic calls from me, saying, "Help, John! The screen just went blank. What did I do wrong?" He *always* had the answer.

Finally, I want to say that every page of this book was written with someone in mind. It is the person for whom life has spiraled out of control. If you are that wounded individual to whom I have been speaking, I pray that God will use my efforts to strengthen you and repair your shattered faith. The Lord is very near—and He cares! So do I.

1

WHEN GOD DOESN'T MAKE SENSE

Chuck Frye was a bright young man of 17, academically gifted and highly motivated. After graduating near the top of his class in high school, he went on to college, where he continued to excel in his studies. Upon completion of his B.S. degree, he applied for admittance to several medical schools. The competition for acceptance was, and is, fierce. At the time, I was a professor at the University of Southern California School of Medicine, where only 106 students were admitted each year out of 6,000 applicants. That was typical of accredited medical programs in that era. Despite these long odds, Chuck was accepted at the University of Arizona School of Medicine and began his formal training in September.

During that first term, Chuck was thinking about the call of God on his life. He began to feel that he should forgo high-tech medicine in some lucrative setting in favor of service on a foreign field. This eventually became his definite plan for the future. Toward the end of that first year of training, however, Chuck was not feeling well. He began experiencing a strange and persistent fatigue. He made an appointment for an examination in May and was soon diagnosed with acute leukemia. Chuck Frye was dead by November.

How could Chuck's heartsick parents then, and how can we now, make sense of this incomprehensible act of God? This young man loved Jesus Christ with all his heart and sought only to do His will. Why was he taken in his prime despite many agonized prayers for his healing by godly family members and faithful friends? The Lord clearly said no to them all. But why?

Thousands of young doctors complete their education every year and enter the medical profession, some for less than admirable reasons. A tiny minority plan to spend their professional lives with the down and outers of the world. But here was a marvelous exception. If permitted to live, Chuck could have treated thousands of poor and needy people who would otherwise suffer and die in utter hopelessness. Not only could he have ministered to their physical needs, but his ultimate desire was to share the gospel with those who had never heard this greatest of stories. Thus, his death simply made no sense. Visualize with me the many desperately ill people Dr. Chuck Frye might have touched in his lifetime, some with cancer, some with tuberculosis, some with congenital disorders, and some too young to even understand their pain. Why would Divine Providence deny them his dedicated service?

There is another dimension to the Frye story that completes the picture. Chuck became engaged to be married in March of that first year in medical school. His fiancée was named Karen Ernst, and she was also a committed believer in Jesus Christ. She learned of Chuck's terminal illness six weeks after their engagement, but she chose to go through with their wedding plans. They became husband and wife in July, less than four months before his tragic death. Karen then enrolled in medical school at the University of Arizona, and after graduation she became a medical missionary in Swaziland in southern Africa. Dr. Frye served there in a church-sponsored hospital until 1992. I'm sure she wonders—amidst so much suffering—why her brilliant young husband was not allowed to fulfill his mission as her medical colleague. And, yes, I wonder too.

The great theologians of the world can contemplate the dilemma posed by Chuck Frye's death for the next 50 years, but they are not likely to produce a satisfying explanation. God's purpose in this young man's demise is a mystery, and there it must remain. Why, after much prayer, was Chuck granted admittance to medical school if he could not live to complete his training? From whence came the missions call to which he responded? Why was so much talent invested in a young man who would not be able to use it? And why was life abbreviated in such a mature and promising student, whereas many drug addicts, winos, and evildoers survive into old age as burdens on society? These troubling questions are much easier to pose than to answer. And there are many others.

The Lord has not yet revealed His reasons for permitting the plane crash that took the lives of my four friends back in 1987. They were among the finest Christian gentlemen I have ever known. Hugo Schoellkopf was an entrepreneur and an extremely able member of the board of directors for Focus on the Family. George Clark was a bank president and a giant of a man. Dr. Trevor Mabrey was a gifted surgeon who performed nearly half of his operations at no charge to his patients. He was a soft touch for anyone with a financial need. And Creath Davis was a minister and author who was loved by thousands. They were close friends who met regularly to study the Word and assure mutual accountability for what they were learning. I loved these four men. I had been with them the night before that last flight, when their twin-engine plane went down in the Absaroka mountain range in Wyoming. There were no survivors. Now their precious wives and children are left to struggle on alone. Why? What purpose was served by their tragic loss? Why are Hugo and Gail's two sons, who are the youngest among the four families, deprived of the influence of their wise and compassionate father during their formative years? I don't know, although the Lord has given Gail sufficient wisdom and strength to carry on alone.

At the first mention of the "awesome why," I think also of our respected friends, Jerry and Mary White. Dr. White is president of the Navigators, a worldwide organization dedicated to knowing Christ and making Him known. The Whites are wonderful people who love the Lord and live by the dictates of Scripture. But they have already had their share of suffering. Their son, Steve, drove a taxi for several months while seeking a career in broadcasting. But he would never achieve his dream. Steve was murdered late one night by a deranged passenger in the usually quiet city of Colorado Springs. The killer was a known felon and drug abuser who had a long history of criminal activity. When he was apprehended, the police learned that he had called for the cab with the intent of shooting whoever arrived to pick him up. Any number of drivers might have responded. Steve White took the call. It was random brutality, beyond any rhyme or reason. And it occurred within a family that had honored and served God for years in full-time Christian service.

I'm reminded of a church in Dallas, Texas, which was destroyed by a tornado some years ago. The twister suddenly dropped from the boiling sky and "selected" this one structure for demolition. Then it lifted again, damaging almost none of the surrounding territory. How would you interpret this "act of God" if you were a member of that congregation? Perhaps the Lord was displeased by something going on in the church, but I doubt if this was His way of showing it. If that is how God deals with disobedience, then sooner or later every sanctuary will be in jeopardy. So how do we explain the selective destruction of the twister? I wouldn't try. There are simply times when things go awry for reasons that may never be understood!

Further examples of inexplicable sorrows and difficulties could fill the shelves of the world's largest library, and every person on earth could contribute illustrations of his or her own. Wars, famines, diseases, natural disasters, and untimely deaths are never easy to rationalize. But large-scale miseries of this nature are sometimes less troubling to the individual than the circumstances that confront each of us personally.

Cancer, kidney failure, heart disease, sudden infant death syndrome, cerebral palsy, Down's syndrome, divorce, rape, loneliness, rejection, failure, infertility, widowhood! These and a million other sources of human suffering produce inevitable questions that trouble the soul. "Why would God permit this to happen to *me?*" It is a question all believers—and many pagans—have struggled to answer. And contrary to Christian teachings in some circles, the Lord typically does not rush in to explain what He is doing.

If you believe God is obligated to explain Himself to us, you ought to examine the following Scriptures. Solomon wrote in Proverbs 25:2, "It is the glory of God to conceal a matter." Isaiah 45:15 states, "Truly you are a God who hides himself." Deuteronomy 29:29 reads, "The secret things belong to the Lord our God." Ecclesiastes 11:5 proclaims, "As you do not know the path of the wind, or how the body is formed in a mother's womb, so you cannot understand the work of God, the Maker of all things." Isaiah 55:8-9 teaches, "'For my thoughts are not your thoughts, neither are your ways my ways,' declares the Lord. 'As the heavens are higher than the earth, so are my ways higher than your ways and my thoughts than your thoughts.'"

Clearly, the Scripture tells us that we lack the capacity to grasp God's infinite mind or the way He intervenes in our lives. How arrogant of us to think otherwise! Trying to analyze His omnipotence is like an amoeba attempting to comprehend the behavior of man. Romans 11:33 (KJV) indicates that God's judgments are "unsearchable" and his ways "past finding out." Similar language is found in 1 Corinthians 2:16: "For who has known the mind of the Lord that he may instruct him?" Clearly, unless the Lord chooses to explain Himself to us, which often He does not, His motivation and purposes are beyond the reach of mortal man. What this means in practical terms is that many of our questions—especially those that begin with the word *why*—will have to remain unanswered for the time being.

The Apostle Paul referred to the problem of unanswered questions when he wrote, "Now we see but a poor reflection as in a mirror; then we shall see face to face. Now I know in part; then I shall know fully, even as I am fully known" (1 Corinthians 13:12). Paul was explaining that we will not have the total picture until we meet in eternity. By implication, we must learn to accept that partial understanding.

Unfortunately, many young believers—and some older ones too—do not know that there will be times in every person's life when circumstances don't add up—when God doesn't appear to make sense. This aspect of the Christian faith is not well advertised. We tend to teach new Christians the portions of our theology that are attractive to a secular mind. For example, Campus Crusade for Christ (an evangelistic ministry I respect highly) has distributed millions of booklets called "The Four Spiritual Laws." The first of those scriptural principles states, "God loves you and offers a wonderful plan for your life." That statement is certainly true. However, it implies that a believer will always comprehend the "wonderful plan" and that he will approve of it. That may not be true.

For some people, such as Joni Eareckson Tada, the "wonderful plan" means life in a wheelchair as a quadriplegic. For others it means early death, poverty, or the scorn of society. For the prophet Jeremiah, it meant being cast into a dark dungeon. For other Bible characters it meant execution. Even in the most terrible of circumstances, however, God's plan is wonderful because anything in harmony with His will ultimately "works for the good of those who love him, who have been called according to his purpose" (Romans 8:28).

Still, it is not difficult to understand how confusion can develop at this point, especially for the young. During the springtime of their years, when health is good and the hardships, failures, and sorrows have not yet blown through their tranquil little world, it is relatively easy to fit the pieces in place. One can honestly believe, with good evidence, that it will always be so. Such a person is extremely vulnerable to spiritual confusion if trouble strikes at that point.

Dr. Richard Selzer is a surgeon and a favorite author of mine. He writes the most beautiful and compassionate descriptions of his patients and the human dramas they confront. In his book *Letters to a Young Doctor,* he said that most of us seem to be protected for a time by an imaginary membrane that shields us from horror. We walk in and through it every day but are hardly aware of its presence. As the immune system protects the human body from the unseen threat of harmful bacteria, so this mythical membrane guards us from life-threatening situations. Not every young person has this protection, of course, because children do die of cancer, congenital heart problems, and other disorders. But most of them are shielded—and don't realize it. Then, as the years roll by, one day it happens. Without warning, the membrane tears and horror seeps into a person's life or into that of a loved one. It is at this moment that an unexpected theological crisis presents itself.

So what am I suggesting—that our heavenly Father is uncaring or unconcerned about His vulnerable sons and daughters, that He taunts us mere mortals as some sort of cruel, cosmic joke? It is almost blasphemous to write such nonsense. Every description given to us in Scripture depicts God as infinitely loving and kind, tenderly watching over His earthly children and guiding the steps of the faithful. He speaks of us as "the people of his pasture, the flock under his care" (Psalm 95:7). This great love led Him to send His only begotten Son as a sacrifice for our sin, that we might escape the punishment we deserve. He did this because He "so loved" the world (John 3:16).

The Apostle Paul expressed it this way: "For I am convinced that neither death nor life, neither angels nor demons, neither the present nor the future, nor any powers, neither height nor depth, nor anything else in all creation, will be able to separate us from the love of God that is in Christ Jesus our Lord" (Romans 8:38-39).

Isaiah conveyed this message to us directly from the heart of the Father: "So do not fear, for I am with you; do not be dismayed, for I am your God. I will strengthen you and help you; I will uphold you with my righteous right hand" (Isaiah 41:10). No, the problem here is not with the love and mercy of God. Nevertheless, the questions persist.

My chief concern at this point, and the reason I have chosen to write this book, is for my fellow believers who are struggling with circumstances that don't make sense. In my work with families who are going through various hardships, from sickness and death to marital conflict and adolescent rebellion, I have found it common for those in crisis to feel great frustration with God. This is particularly true when things happen that seem illogical and inconsistent with what had been taught or understood. Then if the Lord does not rescue them from the circumstances in which they are embroiled, their frustration quickly deteriorates into anger and a sense of abandonment. Finally, disillusionment sets in and the spirit begins to wither.

This can even occur in very young children who are vulnerable to feelings of rejection from God. I'm reminded of a boy named Chris, whose face had been burned in a fire. He sent this note to his psychotherapist:

Dear Dr. Gardner. Some big person, it was a boy about 13, he called me a turtle. And I know he said this because of my plastic surgery. And I think God

*hates me because of my lip. And when I die, he'll
probably send me to hell. Love, Chris.*

Chris naturally concluded that his deformity was
evidence of God's rejection. It is a logical deduction in
the eyes of a child: "If God is all-powerful and He
knows everything, then why would He let such a
terrible thing happen to me? He must hate me."

Unfortunately, Chris is not alone. Many others come
to believe the same satanic lie. In fact, the majority of
us will someday feel a similar alienation from God.
Why? Because those who live long enough will eventually be confronted by happenings they will not understand. That is the human condition. Let me say it again:
It is an incorrect view of Scripture to say that we will
always comprehend what God is doing and how our
suffering and disappointment fit into His plan. Sooner
or later, most of us will come to a point where it appears
that God has lost control—or interest—in the affairs of
people. It is only an illusion, but one with dangerous
implications for spiritual and mental health. Interestingly enough, pain and suffering do not cause the
greatest damage. *Confusion* is the factor that shreds
one's faith.

The human spirit is capable of withstanding enormous discomfort, including the prospect of death, *if the
circumstances make sense*. Many martyrs, political pris-
oners, and war heroes have gone to their graves
willingly and confidently. They understood the sacrifice
they were making and accepted its meaning in their

lives. One is reminded of Nathan Hale moments before he was hanged. He said to his English executioners, "I only regret that I have but one life to lose for my country." Soldiers in battle often die valiantly, even throwing their bodies on live hand grenades to protect their comrades. Others charge deadly machine gun emplacements in order to achieve military objectives. Their attitude appears to be, "The cause for which I'm risking my life is more than justified."

Jim Elliot, one of five missionaries who were speared to death by Auca (now Waorani) people in Ecuador, best described this ultimate investment. He is quoted in Elisabeth Elliot's book *Through Gates of Splendor:* "He is no fool who gives what he cannot keep to gain what he cannot lose." That biblically based understanding turns martyrdom into a glorious victory.

By contrast, Christians who become confused and disillusioned with God have no such consolation. It is the *absence of meaning* that makes their situation so intolerable. As such, their depression over a sudden illness or the tragic death of a loved one can actually be more severe than that experienced by the nonbeliever who expected and received nothing. It is not uncommon to hear a confused Christian express great agitation, anger, or even blasphemy. This confused individual is like a little girl being told by her divorced father that he will come to see her. When Daddy fails to show up, she suffers far more than if he had never offered to come.

The key word here is *expectations*. They set us up for disillusionment. There is no greater distress in human experience than to build one's entire way of life on a certain theological understanding, and then have it collapse at a time of unusual stress and pain. A person in this situation faces the crisis that rattled his foundation. Then, like little Chris, he must also deal with the anguish of rejection. The God whom he has loved, worshiped, and served turns out to appear silent, distant, and uncaring in the moment of greatest need. Do such times come even to the faithful? Yes, they do, although we are seldom willing to admit it within the Christian community.

Wasn't that precisely what happened to Job? This God-fearing man of antiquity had done no wrong, yet he suffered a series of staggering losses in a matter of hours. I have heard many sermons based on the life of this remarkable Old Testament character, but the source of Job's most intense frustration (his inability to find God) has often been overlooked. That is a vital point in the story. Job lost everything—his children, his wealth, his servants, his reputation, and his friends. But those tragedies, as terrible as they were, did not create the greatest agitation for him. Instead, Job fell to the ground in worship and said, "Naked I came from my mother's womb, and naked I will depart. The Lord gave and the Lord has taken away; may the name of the Lord be praised" (Job 1:20-21).

Then God permitted Satan to afflict Job physically. He was stricken "with painful sores from the soles of his feet to the top of his head" (Job 2:7). His wife became irritated and goaded her husband to curse God and die. Job replied, "You are talking like a foolish woman. Shall we accept good from God, and not trouble?" The Scripture then says, "In all this, Job did not sin in what he said" (2:10). What an incredible man of faith! Not even death could shake his confidence, as he proclaimed, "Though he slay me, yet will I hope in him" (13:15).

Eventually, however, Job reached a point of despair. This man of towering strength who had coped with sickness, death, and catastrophic loss soon faced a circumstance that threatened to overwhelm him. It emanated, strangely enough, from his inability to find God. He went through a time when the presence of the Almighty was hidden from view. More important, God wouldn't talk to him. Job expressed his great anguish this way:

> *My complaint is bitter; his hand is heavy in spite of my groaning. If only I knew where to find him; if only I could go to his dwelling! I would state my case before him and fill my mouth with arguments. I would find out what he would answer me, and consider what he would say. Would he oppose me with great power? No, he would not press charges against me. There an upright man could present his case before him, and I would be delivered forever from my judge. But if I go to the east, he is not there; if I go to the west, I do not find him. When he is at work in the north, I do not see him; when he turns to the south, I catch no glimpse of him. (Job 23:2-9)*

Are we to assume that this inability to find and communicate with God in certain times of personal crisis was unique to Job? No, I believe it occurs in many other cases, perhaps to the majority of us at some point in life. Scripture tells us that "no temptation has seized you except what is common to man" (1 Corinthians 10:13). We all go through similar experiences. King David must have felt like Job when he asked the Lord with great passion, "How long, O Lord? Will you forget me forever? How long will you hide your face from me?" (Psalm 13:1). Then in Psalm 77, David again expressed the anguish of his soul: "Will the Lord reject forever? Will he never show his favor again? Has his unfailing love vanished forever?" (vv. 7-8). We're told in 2 Chronicles 32:31 that "God left [Hezekiah] to test him and to know everything that was in his heart." Even Jesus asked why he had been abandoned by God in His final hours on the cross, which ultimately illustrates the experience I am describing.

I am convinced that these and other biblical examples were provided to help us understand a critically important spiritual phenomenon. Apparently, most believers are permitted to go through emotional and spiritual valleys that are designed to test their faith in the crucible of fire. Why? Because faith ranks at the top of God's system of priorities. Without it, He said, it is impossible to please Him (Hebrews 11:6). And what is faith? It is "the substance of things *hoped for, the evidence of things not seen*" (Hebrews 11:1, KJV). This determination to believe when the proof is not provided and when the questions are not answered is central to our relationship with the Lord. He will never do anything to destroy the need for faith. In fact, He guides us through times of testing specifically to cultivate that belief and dependence on Him (Hebrews 11:6-7).

Still, a theological answer of that nature doesn't take away the pain and frustration we experience when we journey through spiritual no-man's-land. And most of us don't handle our difficulties as well as Job or David. When the heat is on and confusion mounts, some believers go through a horrendous spiritual crisis. They "lose God." Doubt rises up to obscure His presence and disillusionment settles into despair. The greatest frustration is knowing that He created the entire universe by simply speaking it into existence, and He has all power and all understanding. He could rescue. He could heal. He could save. But why won't He do it? This sense of abandonment is a terrible experience for someone whose entire being is rooted in the Christian ethic. Satan then drops by for a little visit and whispers, "He is not there! You are alone!"

What does such a person do when God makes no sense? To whom does he confess his troubling—even heretical—thoughts? From whom does he seek counsel? What does he tell his family when his faith is severely shaken? Where does he go to find a new set of values and beliefs? While searching for something more reliable in which to believe, he discovers that there *is* no other name—no other god—to whom he can turn. James 1:8 refers to that individual as a "double minded man [who] is unstable in all his ways" (KJV). He, of all people, is most miserable and confused!

Such a person reminds me of a vine that grew behind the house Shirley and I owned in southern California. It was an ambitious plant that had a secret plan to conquer the world! In its path was a gorgeous, 150-year-old oak tree that I was most anxious to protect. Every few months, I would look out the back window and notice that the vine had again attacked the tree. There it was, winding its way up the trunk and around the upper branches. If allowed to continue, the oak tree would eventually succumb to the invasion of the killer vine!

The solution was really quite simple. Instead of jerking the plant off the tree, which would have damaged the bark, I made one quick cut near the bottom of the vine. Then I walked away. Though nothing appeared to have changed, the green monster had suffered a mortal blow. The next day, its leaves looked a little dull. Two or three days later they were slightly discolored around the edges. Soon they began turning brown with cancerous-looking black spots near the center. Then they started falling off, eventually leaving just a dry stick extending up the trunk. Finally, the stick fell away and the tree stood alone. So much for blind ambition.

Is the analogy clear? Christians who lose God during a period of spiritual confusion are like the vine that has been cut off from its source. They are deprived of nurture and strength. They seem to cope at first, but the concealed wound is mortal. They begin to wither in the heat of the sun. They usually drop out of church and quit reading the Bible and praying. Some go off the deep end and begin doing things they would never have contemplated before. But there is no peace within. Indeed, some of the most bitter, unhappy people on earth are those who have become estranged from the God they no longer understand or trust.

Jesus spoke of this relationship in John 15:5-6 when He said, "I am the vine; you are the branches. If a man remains in me and I in him, he will bear much fruit; apart from me you can do nothing. If anyone does not remain in me, he is like a branch that is thrown away and withers; such branches are picked up, thrown into the fire and burned."

If you are among those people who have been separated from the Vine because of disillusionment or confusion, I have written with you in mind. I know you are hurting. I understand the pain that engulfed you when your child died or your husband betrayed you or your beloved wife went to be with Jesus. You could not explain the devastating earthquake, or the fire, or the terrible tornado, or the unseasonable rainstorm that ruined your crops. The insurance company said it was an "act of God." Yes. That's what hurt the most. The examples are endless. I'm thinking of a young man I know who was convinced the Lord would let him have the girl he desperately loved. He thought he could not live without her. The day she married another man, his faith was shaken to its foundation.

I'm reminded also of the woman who called in 1991

to tell me that her 28-year-old son had been killed in the Persian Gulf War. He was in a helicopter that was shot down somewhere in Iraq. He was her only son and was a born-again Christian. Only a handful of the 600,000 United Nations troops in that war failed to come home alive, yet this God-fearing man was one of them. My heart aches for his grieving mother.

The great danger for people who have experienced this kind of tragedy is that Satan will use their pain to make them feel victimized by God. What a deadly trap that is! When a person begins to conclude that he or she is disliked or hated by the Almighty, demoralization is not far behind.

For the heartsick, bleeding soul out there today who is desperate for a word of encouragement, let me assure you that you *can* trust this Lord of heaven and earth. There is security and rest in the wisdom of the eternal Scriptures. We will discuss those comforting passages in subsequent chapters, and I believe you will see that the Lord can be trusted—even when He can't be tracked. Of this you can be certain: Jehovah, King of kings and Lord of lords, is not pacing the corridors of heaven in confusion over the problems in your life! He hung the worlds in space. He can handle the burdens that have weighed you down, and he cares about you deeply. For a point of beginning He says, "Be still, and know that I am God" (Psalm 46:10).

2

THE BETRAYAL BARRIER

I heard a story many years ago about a man who was driving his truck on a narrow mountain road. To his right was a cliff that dropped precipitously nearly 500 feet to a canyon below. As the driver rounded a curve, he suddenly lost control of the vehicle. It plunged over the side and bounced down the mountain, bursting into flames at the bottom. Although the terrified man was ejected as his truck went over the edge, he managed to grab a bush that grew near the top. There he was, frantically holding the small limb and dangling precariously over the abyss. After trying to pull himself up for several minutes, he called out in desperation, "Is anybody there?"

In a few seconds, the thundering voice of the Lord echoed across the mountain. "Yes, I am here," He said. "What do you want?"

The man pleaded, "Please save me! I can't hold on much longer!"

After another agonizing pause, the voice said, "All right. I will save you. But first you must turn loose of the limb and trust Me to catch you. Just release your grip now. My hands will be under you."

The dangling man looked over his shoulder at the burning truck in the valley below, and then he called out, "Is anybody *else* there?"

Have you ever found yourself in a similar fix? Have

you ever pleaded for God's help in a distressful situation and had Him ask you to trust Him with your life? Have you ever weighed His reply and then wanted to ask, "Is anybody *else* there?" As we have indicated, that is not an uncommon experience in this Christian walk. We think we know what we need in a moment of crisis, but God often has other ideas.

After years of consistent answers to prayers, the Lord may choose not to grant a request we think is vitally important. In a matter of moments, the world can fall off its axis. Panic stalks the soul as life and death hang in the balance. A pounding heart betrays the anxiety within. "But where is God? Does He know what is happening? Is He concerned? Why have the heavens grown dark and silent? What have I done to deserve this abandonment? Haven't I served Him with a willing heart? What must I do to regain His favor?" Then, as frustration and fear accumulate, the human spirit recoils in distrust and confusion.

I wish I had the words to explain the full measure of this experience. Indeed, from my 26 years of professional counseling, I have seen few other circumstances in living that equal the agony of a shattered faith. It is a crisis brewed in the pit of hell. Dr. R. T. Kendall, the gifted senior minister of Westminster Chapel in London, said it leads directly to what he calls "the betrayal barrier." In his opinion, 100 percent of believers eventually go through a period when God seems to let them down. It may occur shortly after becoming a Christian. The new convert loses his job, or his child becomes ill, or business reverses occur. Or maybe after serving Him faithfully for many years, life suddenly starts to unravel. It makes no sense. It seems so unfair. The natural reaction is to say, "Lord, is *this* the way You treat Your own? I thought You cared for me, but I was wrong. I can't love a God like that." It is a tragic misunderstanding.

Scripture is replete with examples of this troubling human experience. We see it illustrated in Exodus 5, when God commanded Moses to appeal to Pharaoh for the release of the children of Israel. Moses did as he was told, after which the ruler angrily increased his oppression of the people, beating them and forcing them to work even harder. The people sent a delegation to Pharaoh in hopes of getting some relief. But Pharaoh was in no mood to negotiate. He called them "lazy" and ordered them to get back to work—or else. The men left the palace visibly shaken and ran straight into Moses and Aaron. They said, "May the Lord look upon you and judge you! You have made us a stench to Pharaoh and his officials and have put a sword in their hand to kill us" (Exodus 5:21).

Moses had good reason to feel God had pushed him out on a limb and abandoned him there. He reacted as you or I would under the circumstances. The Scripture tells us he said, "O Lord, why have you brought trouble upon this people? Is this why you sent me? Ever since I went to Pharaoh to speak in your name, he has brought trouble upon this people, and you have not rescued your people at all" (Exodus 5:22-23).

We can see today how Moses misinterpreted what God was doing, but who can blame him? He appeared to be the victim of a cruel joke. Fortunately, Moses clung to his faith until he began to understand the plan. Most of us lesser mortals do not do as well. We bail out before the pieces start fitting together. Forever after, we're disillusioned and hurt. Dr. Kendall said more than 90 percent of us fail to break through this betrayal barrier after feeling abandoned by God. Our faith is then hindered by a bitter experience that we can't forget.

Dr. Kendall's observation is consistent with my own. Many people who want to serve the Lord are victimized by a terrible lie that distances them from the Giver of Life. Satan is, as we know, both the "father of lies" (John 8:44) and "a roaring lion looking for someone to devour" (1 Peter 5:8). It is his specific purpose to discourage us and distort the truth. He can usually be expected to show up at the moment of greatest discouragement, whispering his wicked thoughts and taunting the wounded believer.

For the benefit of those of you who are enduring that withering attack on your faith, I want to share some similar experiences in the lives of other Christians. As indicated, it is important to recognize that you are not alone. Your pain and discouragement, which might lead you to ask "Why *me?*" are not unique. You have not been singled out for sorrow. Most of us are destined, it seems, to bump our heads on the same ol' rock. From ancient times, men and women have grieved over stressful circumstances that did not fit any pattern of logic or symmetry. It happens to us all sooner or later. Millions have been there. And despite what some Christians will tell you, being a follower of Jesus Christ is no foolproof insurance policy against these storms of life.

Consider, for example, the life and death of Dr. Paul Carlson. In 1961, he had joined a relief agency to serve as a medical missionary in the Belgian Congo. It was only a six-month commitment, but what he saw there changed his life. He could not forget the hopeless people when he returned to his thriving medical practice in Redondo Beach, California. He told a colleague, "If you could only see [the need], you wouldn't be able to swallow your sandwich." Soon, Dr. Carlson moved his family to Africa and set up a makeshift clinic, operating at times by flashlight and making house calls on his motorbike. His salary dropped to $3,230 per year, but money didn't matter. He was marching to a different drummer.

Two years later, however, Dr. Carlson became a pawn in a bloody confrontation between rival revolutionary factions in the Belgian Congo. He was among a small band of Americans who were held captive near the battle zone. They had one fleeting opportunity to escape by scaling a wall and dropping to safety on the other side. Dr. Carlson reached the top of the barrier and was a split second from freedom when a burst of bullets tore through his body. He fell back into the courtyard and died. It was a senseless killing by rebels who had nothing to gain by his murder.

Time magazine, in its report of the killing, said this about the physician:

> *Dr. Carlson's murder, along with the massacre of perhaps another hundred whites and thousands of blacks, had a special, tragic meaning. [He] symbolized all the white men—and there are many—who want nothing from Africa but a chance to help. He was no saint and no deliberate martyr. He was a highly skilled physician who, out of a strong Christian faith and a sense of common humanity, had gone to the Congo to treat the sick.*[1]

That humanitarian commitment cost Dr. Paul Earle Carlson his life.

And we are left to ask, "Why, Lord? Why couldn't You have distracted the gunner for another instant?" Even a butterfly in front of his nose or some sweat in his eyes could have changed the tragic outcome. No such distraction occurred. And so ended the earthly days of a good man who left a loving wife and two children behind.

How about the experience of my friends Daryl and Clarita Gustafson? They were infertile for many years, despite exhaustive medical tests and procedures. They prayed consistently for God to grant them the privilege

1 "The World, Africa, The Congo Massacre," *Time* (December 4, 1964).

of bringing a child into the world, but the heavens were silent and the womb remained barren. The ticking of Clarita's biological clock was deafening as the months slid into history. Then one day it happened. Clarita discovered that she was gloriously pregnant. God had spoken at last. A healthy baby boy was born seven months later, and he was named Aaron, after Moses' brother. This child was their pride and joy.

When Aaron was three years old, however, he was diagnosed as having a very virulent form of cancer. What followed were 10 months of painful chemotherapy and radiation treatment. Despite all efforts to arrest the disease, Aaron's little body continued to deteriorate. His mother and father vacillated between hope and despair, as only the parents of dying children can fully comprehend. Despite many prayers and countless tears, Aaron went to be with the Lord in 1992, at four years of age. Thus, the miracle child, whom Daryl and Clarita called "God's little angel and our little pumpkin," was taken from them. The faith of this remarkable family has remained strong, although their questions still have not been answered.

My heart aches for these and all the other mothers and fathers who have lost a precious child. Indeed, I hear regularly from parents who have experienced a similar tragedy. One family, in particular, stands out in my mind. I learned of their sorrow from the father who sent me a tribute to the memory of his little girl, Bristol. This is what he wrote:

My Dear Bristol,

Before you were born I prayed for you. In my heart I knew that you would be a little angel. And so you were.

When you were born on my birthday, April 7, it was evident that you were a special gift from the Lord. But how profound a gift you turned out to be! More than the beautiful bundle of gurgles and rosy cheeks—more than the first-born of my flesh, a joy unspeakable—you showed me God's love more than anything else in all creation. Bristol, you taught me how to love.

I certainly loved you when you were cuddly and cute, when you rolled over and sat up and jabbered your first words. I loved you when the searing pain of realization took hold that something was wrong—that maybe you were not developing as quickly as your peers, and then when we understood it was more serious than that. I loved you when we went from hospital to clinic to doctor looking for a medical diagnosis that would bring some hope. And, of course, we always prayed for you—and prayed—and prayed. I loved you when one of the tests resulted in too much spinal fluid being drawn from your body and you screamed. I loved you when you moaned and cried, when your mom and I and your sisters would drive for hours late at night to help you fall asleep. I loved you with tears in my eyes when, confused, you would bite your fingers or your lip by accident, and when your eyes crossed and then went blind.

I most certainly loved you when you could no longer speak, but how profoundly I missed your voice! I loved you when your scoliosis started wrenching your body like a pretzel, when we put a tube in your stomach so you could eat because you were choking on your food, which we fed you one spoonful at a time for up to two hours per meal. I managed to love you when your contorted limbs would not allow ease of changing your messy diapers—so many diapers—ten years of diapers. Bristol, I even loved you when you could not say the one thing in life that I longed to hear back—"Daddy, I love you." Bristol, I loved you when I was close to God and when He seemed far away, when I was full of faith and also when I was angry at Him.

And the reason I loved you, my Bristol, in spite of these difficulties, is that God put this love in my heart. This is the wondrous nature of God's love, that he loves us even when we are blind, deaf, or twisted—in body or in spirit. God loves us even when we can't tell Him that we love Him back.

My dear Bristol, now you are free! I look forward to that day, according to God's promises, when we will be joined together with you with the Lord, completely whole and full of joy. I'm so happy that you have your crown first. We will follow you some-day—in His time.

Before you were born I prayed for you. In my

heart I knew that you would be a little angel. And so you were!

Love, Daddy

Though I have never met this loving father, I personally identify with the passion of his heart. What an understatement! I can still hardly read his words without fighting back tears. I've had the same tenderness toward my son and daughter since the day they were born. Even with this empathy, I can only begin to imagine the agony wrought by the 10-year ordeal described in this dad's letter. Not only is this kind of tragedy an emotional nightmare, but it can become the spiritual mine field I have described.

Again, these examples of heartache illustrate the fact that godly people—praying people—sometimes face the same hardships that nonbelievers experience. If we deny that fact, we create even greater pain and disillusionment for those who are unprepared to handle it. That is why we must overcome our reluctance to admit these unpleasant realities. We must brace our brothers and sisters against the betrayal barrier. We must teach them not to depend too heavily on their own ability to comprehend the inexplicable circumstances in our lives.

Remember that the Scripture warns us to "lean not on your own understanding" (Proverbs 3:5). Note that we are not prohibited from trying to understand. I've spent a lifetime attempting to get a handle on some of the imponderables of life, which has led to the writing of this book. But we are specifically told not to *lean* on our ability to make the pieces fit. "Leaning" refers to the panicky demand for answers—throwing faith to the wind if a satisfactory response cannot be produced. It is pressing God to explain Himself—or else! That is where everything starts to unravel.

Admittedly, I do not have tidy answers that will satisfy Aaron's parents, or Mrs. Carlson, or Dr. Karen Frye. I have no airtight explanations for Bristol's aching father or the parents of Steve White. In fact, I find it irritating when amateur theologians throw around simplistic platitudes, such as "God must have wanted the little flower named Bristol for His heavenly garden." Nonsense! A loving Father does not tear the heart out of a family for selfish purposes! No, it is better to acknowledge that we have been given too few facts to explain all the heartache in an imperfect, fallen world. That understanding will have to await the coming of the sovereign Lord who promises to set straight all accounts and end all injustice.

If you have begun to slide into despondency, it is extremely important to take a new look at Scripture and recognize that trials and suffering are part of the human condition. All of the biblical writers, including the giants of the faith, went through similar hardships. Look at the experience of Joseph, one of the patriarchs of the Old Testament. His entire life was in shambles until the triumphal reunion with his family many years later. He was hated by his brothers, who considered killing him before selling him as a slave. While in Egypt, he was imprisoned, falsely accused of attempted rape by Poti-phar's wife, and threatened with execution. There is no indication that God explained to Joseph what He was doing through those many years of heartache, or how the pieces would eventually fit together. He was ex-pected, like you and me, to live out his days one at a time in something less than complete understanding. What pleased God was Joseph's faithfulness when nothing made sense.

Consider the account of Elijah in 1 Kings 17. In the third verse we learn that God is telling him to "leave here, turn eastward and hide in the Kerith Ravine, east of the Jordan. You will drink from the brook, and I have ordered the ravens to feed you there." That was good news because of the great drought in the land at the time. At least he would not die of thirst. But then we read in verse 7, "Some time later the brook dried up because there had been no rain in the land." What a strange thing to happen! Do you suppose Elijah was thinking, *You sent me here, Lord, and promised me food and water. So why did You let the brook run dry?* Good question. Has the source of God's blessing in your life ever run dry?

Let's zip over to the New Testament and look at the disciples and other early Christian leaders. John the Baptist, of whom Jesus said there was no greater man born of woman, found himself in Herod's stinking dungeon. There an evil woman named Herodias had him beheaded in revenge because he had condemned her immoral conduct. There is no record in Scripture that an angel visited John's cell to explain the meaning of his persecution. This great, godly man, who was the designated forerunner to Jesus, went through the same confusing experiences as we. It is comforting to know that John responded in a very human way. He sent a secret message to Jesus from his prison cell asking, "Are you the one who was to come, or should we expect someone else?" (Matthew 11:3). Have you ever felt like asking that question?

Look at the martyrdom of Stephen, who was stoned to death for proclaiming the name of Christ. And the disciple James, to whom Acts 12 devotes only one verse: King Herod Agrippa "had James, the brother of John, put to death with the sword" (Acts 12:2). Tradition tells us that 10 of the 12 disciples were eventually executed (excluding Judas, who committed suicide, and John, who was exiled). We also believe that Paul, who was persecuted, stoned, and flogged, was later beheaded in a Roman prison. The second half of Hebrews chapter 11 describes some of those who suffered for the name of Christ:

> *Others were tortured and refused to be released, so that they might gain a better resurrection. Some faced jeers and flogging, while still others were chained and put in prison. They were stoned; they were sawed in two; they were put to death by the sword. They went about in sheepskins and goatskins, destitute, persecuted and mistreated—the world was not worthy of them. They wandered in*

deserts and mountains, and in caves and holes in the ground. These were all commended for their faith, yet none of them received what had been promised. (Hebrews 11:35-39)

Read that last verse again. Note that these saints lived in anticipation of a promise that had not been fulfilled by the time of their deaths. A full explanation never came. They had only their faith to hold them steady in their time of persecution. The *Life Application Bible Commentary* says of this chapter, "These verses summarize the lives of other great men and women of faith. Some experienced outstanding victories, even over the threat of death. But others were severely mistreated, tortured, and even killed. Having a steadfast faith in God does not guarantee a happy, carefree life. On the contrary, our faith almost guarantees us some form of abuse from the world. While we are on earth, we may never see the purpose of our suffering. But we know that God will keep ~~his~~ promises to us." *That* is precisely the point.

Few of us are called upon to lay down our lives like those of the early church, but modern-day examples do exist. Try explaining this one: Rev. Bill Hybels shared an experience in his book *Too Busy Not to Pray* that speaks dramatically to this issue:

A couple of years ago, a member of my church's vocal team and I were invited by a Christian leader named Yesu to go to southern India. There we joined a team of people from various parts of the U.S. We were told that God would use us to reach Muslims and Hindus and nonreligious people for Christ. We all felt called by God to go, but none of us knew what to expect.

When we arrived, Yesu met us and invited us to his home. Over the course of the next few days, he told us about his ministry.

Yesu's father, a dynamic leader and speaker, had started the mission in a Hindu-dominated area. One day a Hindu leader came to Yesu's father and asked for prayer. Eager to pray with him, hoping he would lead him to Christ, he took him into a private room, knelt down with him, closed his eyes and began to pray. While he was praying, the Hindu man reached into his robe, pulled out a knife and stabbed him repeatedly.

Yesu, hearing his father's screams, ran to help him. He held him in his arms as blood poured out onto the floor of the hut. Three days later, his father died. On his deathbed he said to his son, "Please tell that man that he is forgiven. Care for your mother and carry on this ministry. Do whatever it takes to win people to Christ."

What an inspiring and humbling story! It makes me feel ashamed for complaining about the petty problems and frustrations I have encountered through the years. Someday, the Lord may require a similar sacrifice of me in the cause of Christ. If so, I pray I will have the courage to accept *whatever* His will is for me. Untold multitudes have dedicated their lives to His service in this manner.

So tell me, where did we get the notion that the Christian life is a piece of cake? Where is the evidence for the "name it, claim it" theology that promises God will skip along in front of us with His great Cosmic Broom, sweeping aside each trial and every troubling uncertainty? To the contrary, Jesus told His disciples that they should anticipate suffering. He said, "I have told you these things, so that in me you may have peace. In this world you will have trouble. But take heart! I have overcome the world" (John 16:33). Paul wrote, "In all our troubles my joy knows no bounds. For when we came into Macedonia, this body of ours had no rest, but we were harassed at every turn—conflicts on the outside, fears within" (2 Corinthians 7:4-5). Peter left no doubt about difficulties in this Christian life when he wrote, "Dear friends, do not be surprised at the painful trial you are suffering, as though something strange were happening to you. But rejoice that you participate in the sufferings of Christ, so that you may be overjoyed when his glory is revealed" (1 Peter 4:12-13). Note in each of these references the coexistence of both joy and pain.

This is the consistent, unequivocal "expectation" that we have been given by the biblical writers, and yet we seem determined to rewrite the text. That makes us sitting ducks for satanic mischief.

My concern is that many believers apparently feel

God owes them smooth sailing or at least a full explanation (and perhaps an apology) for the hardships they encounter. We must never forget that He, after all, is *God*. He is majestic and holy and sovereign. He is accountable to no one. He is not an errand boy who chases the assignments we dole out. He is not a genie who pops out of the bottle to satisfy our whims. He is not our servant—we are His. And our reason for existence is to glorify and honor Him. Even so, sometimes He performs mighty miracles on our behalf. Sometimes He chooses to explain His action in our lives. Sometimes His presence is as real as if we had encountered Him face to face. But at other times when nothing makes sense—when what we are going through is "not fair," when we feel all alone in God's waiting room—He simply says, "Trust Me!"

Does this mean that we are destined to be depressed and victimized by the circumstances of our lives? Certainly not. Paul said we are "more than conquerors." He wrote in Philippians 4:4-7:

> *Rejoice in the Lord always. I will say it again: Rejoice! Let your gentleness be evident to all. The Lord is near. Do not be anxious about anything, but in everything, by prayer and petition, with thanksgiving, present your requests to God. And the peace of God, which transcends all understanding, will guard your hearts and your minds in Christ Jesus.*

Clearly, what we have in Scripture is a paradox. On the one hand, we are told to expect suffering and hardship that could even cost us our lives. On the other hand, we are encouraged to be joyful, thankful, and "of good cheer." How do those contradictory ideas link together? How can we be triumphant and under intense pressure at the same time? How can we be secure when surrounded by insecurity? That is a mystery which, according to Paul, "transcends all understanding."

In the next chapter, we'll discuss the principles that lead to this uncanny peace of mind in the midst of the storm. It is available in your life too.

3

GOD MAKES
SENSE EVEN
WHEN HE
DOESN'T
MAKE SENSE

I have been thinking for many years about those occasions when God doesn't make sense. I was in my late teens when the first "awesome why" came rocketing through my brain. I don't remember today what precipitated that troublesome thought, but I knew I had hit an issue that required more horsepower than I possessed. I've now had a little more time—well, maybe more than a little—to study the Word and sort out my frame of reference. Some 53 years have come and gone since I gave my heart to Jesus Christ as a three-year-old child. I am still committed to this Master with every fiber of my being, and that conviction is deeper and stronger today than it has ever been.

Furthermore, this passage of time and the counsel of some biblical scholars have helped me come to terms with what I believe is the correct understanding of those periods when faith is severely challenged. I believe I have gotten a better idea of who God is and how He interacts with us—especially in four specific areas.

1. God is present and involved in our lives even when He seems deaf or on an extended leave of absence.

When I was a boy, I heard a mystery program on radio that captured my imagination. It told the story of a man who was condemned to solitary confinement in a pitch-black cell. The only thing he had to occupy his mind was a marble, which he threw repeatedly against the walls. He spent his hours listening to the marble as it bounced and rolled around the room. Then he would grope in the darkness until he found his precious toy.

One day, the prisoner threw his marble upward—but it failed to come down. Only silence echoed through the darkness. He was deeply disturbed by the "evaporation" of the marble and his inability to explain its disappearance. Finally he went berserk, pulled out all his hair, and died.

When the prison officials came to remove his body, a guard noticed something caught in a huge spider's web in the upper corner of the room.

That's strange, he thought. *I wonder how a marble got up there.*

As the story of the frantic prisoner illustrates, human perception sometimes poses questions the mind is incapable of answering. But valid answers always exist. For those of us who are followers of Jesus Christ, it just makes good sense not to depend too heavily on our ability to make the pieces fit—especially when we're trying to figure out the Almighty!

Not only is human perception a highly flawed and imprecise instrument, but our emotions are even less reliable. They have the consistency and dependability of Silly Putty. I wrote a book some years ago entitled, *Emotions: Can You Trust Them?* I invested nearly 200 pages to answer my own question in the negative. No, we can't depend on our feelings and passions to govern our lives or assess the world around us. Emotions are unreliable—biased—whimsical. They lie as often as they tell the truth. They are manipulated by hormones—especially in the teen years—and they wobble dramatically from early morning, when we're rested, to the evening, when we're tired. One of the evidences of emotional maturity is the ability (and the willingness) to overrule ephemeral feelings and govern our behavior with the intellect and the will. (Did it really require 200 pages to say *that?*)

If perceptions or emotions are suspect at best, then we must be extremely wary in accepting what they tell us about God. Unfortunately, many believers seem unaware of this source of confusion and disillusionment. It is typical for vulnerable people to accept what they "feel" about the Lord at face value. But what they feel may reflect nothing more than a momentary frame of mind. Furthermore, the mind, the body, and the spirit are very close neighbors. One usually catches the ills of the next. If a person is depressed, for example, it affects not only his emotional and physical well-being; his spiritual life suffers too. He may conclude, "God doesn't love me. I just don't feel His approval." Likewise, the first thing an individual is likely to say when diagnosed with a threatening physical illness is, "Why would God do this to me?" These three faculties are inextricably linked, and they weaken the objectivity of our perception.

This understanding becomes extremely important when it comes to evaluating our relationship with God. Even when He seems 1,000 miles away and uninterested in our affairs, He is close enough to touch. A wonderful illustration of this unseen presence is described in Luke 24, verses 13 and 14, when two of Jesus' disciples were walking toward a village called Emmaus, about seven miles from Jerusalem. They had seen their Master horribly crucified three days earlier, and they were severely depressed. Everything that they hoped for had died on that Roman cross. All the dramatic things Jesus had said and done now appeared contrived and untrue. He had spoken with such authority, but now He was dead and laid to rest in a borrowed tomb. He claimed to be the Son of God, yet they had heard Him cry in His last hours, "My God, my God, why have you forsaken me?" (Matthew 27:46). The disciples couldn't have been more confused. What was the meaning of the time they had spent with this man who called Himself the Messiah?

What they didn't realize was that Jesus was walking that dusty road with them at that very moment, and that they were about to be given the greatest news ever heard by human ears. It would revolutionize their lives and turn the rest of the world upside down. At the time, however, all they saw were facts that could not be harmonized. They had, I submit, a problem of *perception*.

In my work with Christian families in crisis, I find them struggling in many of the same ways as the disciples. As they trudge along in deep thought, there is no evidence that Jesus is in their part of the universe. Because they don't "feel" His presence, they cannot believe He cares. Since the facts don't add up, they are convinced no reasonable explanation exists. Their prayers bring no immediate relief, so they presume they are not heard. But they are wrong. It is my firm conviction in these instances that too much confidence is placed in what people feel, and too little on the promises of God, who said He would supply all our needs according to His riches in glory by Christ Jesus (Philippians 4:19).

If you find yourself on that dusty road to Emmaus today, and the circumstances in your life have left you confused and depressed, I have a word of counsel for you. Never assume God's silence or apparent inactivity is evidence of His disinterest. Let me say it again. Feelings about His inaccessibility mean nothing! Absolutely nothing! His Word is infinitely more reliable than our spooky emotions. Rev. Reubin Welch, minister and author, once said, "With God, even when nothing is happening—*something* is happening." It is true. The Lord is at work in His own unique way even when our prayers seem to echo back from an empty universe.

Establish your foundation not on ephemeral emotions but on the authority of the written Word. He promised never to leave us (Matthew 28:20). He said, "For where two or three come together in my name, there am I with them" (Matthew 18:20). He is "a friend who sticks closer than a brother" (Proverbs 18:24). We're assured that "the eyes of the Lord are on the righteous and his ears are attentive to their prayer" (1 Peter 3:12). David said:

Where can I go from your Spirit? Where can I flee from your presence? If I go up to the heavens, you are there; if I make my bed in the depths, you are there. If I rise on the wings of the dawn, if I settle on the far side of the sea, even there your hand will guide me, your right hand will hold me fast. (Psalm 139:7-10)

These promises and proclamations remain true even if we have no spiritual feelings whatsoever. Cling to that truth with the tenacity of a bulldog! For, as Kierkegaard said, "Faith is holding onto uncertainties with passionate conviction."

2. God's timing is perfect, even when He appears catastrophically late.

One of the greatest destroyers of faith is *timing* that doesn't fit our preconceived notions. We live in a fast-paced world where we have come to expect instant responses to every desire and need. Instant coffee. Instant potatoes. Instant cash from the little money machine. Instant relief for sore muscles and minor backache. It's almost our birthright to make the world jump at our demands. But God doesn't operate that way. He is never in a hurry. And sometimes, He can be agonizingly slow in solving the problems we bring to His attention. It's almost enough to make an impatient believer give up and try something else.

Before bailing out, however, we should take another look at the story of Mary, Martha, and their brother,

Lazarus, as told in John 11. The members of this little family were among Jesus' closest friends during the time of His earthly ministry. Verse 5 says, "Jesus loved Martha and her sister and Lazarus." It was reasonable, given this affection, for them to expect certain favors from Jesus—especially if life-threatening emergencies ever occurred. Indeed, they were soon confronted by precisely that situation when Lazarus became desperately ill. His sisters did the logical thing—they sent an urgent note to Jesus, saying, "Lord, the one you love is sick" (v. 3). They had every reason to believe He would respond.

Mary and Martha waited and watched the road for Jesus' appearance, but He did not come. Hours dragged into anxious days with no sign of the Master. Meanwhile, Lazarus was steadily losing ground. He was obviously dying. But where in the world was Jesus? Did He get the message? Didn't He know the seriousness of the illness? Didn't He care? As the sisters sat vigilantly at his bedside, Lazarus soon closed his eyes in death.

The sisters were grief stricken. Also, they must have been extremely frustrated with Jesus. He was out there somewhere performing miracles for total strangers, opening blind eyes and healing the lame. Yet here they were in critical need of His care, and He was too busy to come. I can imagine Mary and Martha saying quietly to each other, "I just don't understand. I thought He loved us. Why would He abandon us like this?" They wrapped Lazarus in graveclothes and conducted a sad little funeral. Jesus did not attend. Then they said good-bye to their brother and lovingly placed his body in a tomb.

Mary and Martha loved Jesus with all their hearts, but it would have been reasonable for them to have been annoyed when He showed up four days later. They may have been tempted to say, "Where have You been, Sir? We tried to tell You that Your friend was dying, but we couldn't get Your attention. Well, You're too late now. You could have saved Him, but apparently there were more important things on Your mind." Mary's actual words were much more respectful, of course. What she said was, "Lord, . . . if you had been here, my brother would not have died" (John 11:21). She wept as she spoke and the Lord was "deeply moved in spirit and troubled" (v. 33).

Jesus then performed one of His most dramatic miracles as He called Lazarus out of the tomb. You see, the Master was not really late at all. He only appeared to be overdue. He arrived at the precise moment necessary to fulfill the purposes of God—just as He always does.

With no disrespect intended, let me say that what happened there in Bethany is characteristic of the Christian life. Haven't you noticed that Jesus usually shows up about four days late? He often arrives after we have wept and worried and paced the floor—after we have sweated out the medical examination or fretted our way through business reverses. If He had arrived on time we could have avoided much of the stress that occurred in His absence. Yet it is extremely important to recognize that He is never actually late.

His timetable for action is simply different from ours. And it is usually slower!

Let me illustrate this concept from my own experience. In 1985 I was asked by the United States Attorney General, Edwin Meese, to serve on his Commission on Pornography. It was without doubt the most difficult and unpleasant assignment of my life. For 18 months, the 10 other members and I handled a thankless and nauseating responsibility. We traveled extensively and examined the most wretched magazines, books, films, and videotapes in existence anywhere in the world. Since the United States is the fountainhead for obscenity worldwide, we were immersed in this filth for what seemed like an eternity. Furthermore, the pornographers and smut peddlers tracked our commission like a pack of wolves following a herd of caribou. They did everything they could to intimidate and humiliate us.

I remember sitting in the public hearings day after day with various types of cameras, including videos, aimed at my face. I could see my reverse image reflected in their lenses for hours, which tends to make one self-conscious. The photographers were waiting for me to do something embarrassing, such as make a weird face or put my finger near my nose. One day when I stood up to leave for a lunch break, I turned around and was confronted by a photographer and his clicking camera just inches from my face. Always, there were microphones taped beside my place at the table to record every whispered word or remark. My comments were then parodied the following month in various pornographic publications. *Hustler* magazine superimposed my picture on the backside of a donkey, awarding me the title Ass___ of the Month. The attorney general never said it would be easy.

These efforts at harassment were momentary irritants. Bigger guns would be rolled out later, and they were fired soon enough. A $30 million lawsuit was filed by three organizations, *Playboy, Penthouse,* and the American Magazine Association, shortly before we issued our final report. It named as defendants every member of the commission, its executive director (Alan Sears), and Attorney General Edwin Meese. The complaint was a trumped-up bit of legalese that our lawyers said was totally without merit. Attorneys at the Department of Justice told us not to worry—the case should be thrown out of court in short order. They were wrong.

The matter was assigned to Judge John Garrett Penn, one of the most liberal judges in the Northeast. Incredibly, he held the ridiculous case on his desk for more than two years before ruling on a relatively simple motion for summary judgment. Eventually, he decided in our favor. The litigants immediately appealed, and we spent another year in limbo. We won the next round, which was followed by yet another appeal. For six years this threatening suit hung over our heads as it worked its way through the legal system. It finally reached the Supreme Court in early 1992, which thankfully ended the ordeal. This is the way 11 citizens were rewarded for serving without compensation at the request of their country!

Getting back to our theme, Shirley and I prayed about the lawsuit when it was filed back in 1986. I was carrying heavy responsibilities at Focus on the Family and certainly didn't need this distraction. We asked that the "cup" be removed from us, but there was no immediate reply from the Lord. Thus, the process was allowed to run its course with its inevitable drain on my physical and emotional resources. Six years later, Jesus "showed up" and the issue was resolved. But why, I wondered, did He come "four days late"? Was there anything gained by dragging out the case in the courts? I'm sure there was, knowing that every prayer is answered either positively or negatively. I also believe literally that "in all things God works for the good of those who love him, who have been called according to his purpose" (Romans 8:28). Nevertheless, I am unable to explain or understand why I had to go through six years of wasted time and energy to settle this irritant. But then, it really doesn't matter, does it? It is unnecessary for me to be told why the Lord permitted the suit to continue. As long as I know He loves me and He never makes a mistake, why should I not be content to rest in His protection?

From my study of the Scriptures and from personal experiences such as the one cited above, I have drawn the conclusion that God's economy of time and energy is very different from ours. Most of us in Western nations are motivated to use every second of our existence for some gainful purpose. But the Lord sometimes permits our years to be "squandered," or so it would seem, without a backward glance. It is difficult to understand, for example, why He dealt with young David as He did. This shepherd boy was hand-selected by the Lord from all the youths of Israel to succeed Saul as King. Not even David's father, Jesse, could believe his seven other sons were passed over in favor of the youngest. Yet David was designated as the future patriarch of Israel. What an auspicious beginning for an adolescent tender of sheep.

But take another look. God then permitted Saul to chase David into the wilderness where he spent 14 years running for his life. From a human perspective, this time as a fugitive was an enormous waste of David's youthful years. He could have been sent through a training program to prepare him for national leadership or any number of worthwhile endeavors. Almost anything would have been more profitable, it seems, than sitting around a campfire telling war stories and wondering where Saul and his band of merry men would pop up. He must have despaired of ever going home again. But the Lord had David right where He wanted Him. Obviously, there is no "tyranny of the urgent" in God's scheme of things. He acts according to His own ordered schedule. Even Jesus, who lived 33 years on earth, spent only three in active ministry! Think of how many more people He could have healed—and how many more divine truths He could have imparted—in another decade or two.

Look at the human talent that has been "wasted" by early death or disability over the centuries. Wolfgang Mozart, for example, may have had the greatest musical mind in the history of the world. He composed his first symphony at five years of age and turned out a remarkable volume of brilliant work. But he died penniless at 35, being unable to attract any interest in his compositions. His most valuable possession at the time of his death was a violin worth about two dollars. He was buried in an unmarked pauper's grave, and no one attended his funeral. Who was it that said life is fair?

Although I'm aware of no evidence that Mozart was a believer, I still find it interesting to contemplate the Lord's role in his early demise. Just imagine the music Mozart could have written if permitted to live another 20 or 30 years. Wouldn't you enjoy hearing the "best of the never written symphonies" that might have come from this maturing genius? How about Ludwig van Beethoven, who began losing his hearing before he was 30 years of age? Consider the great Christian leaders who were taken before they had exhausted their potential, such as Oswald Chambers who died at 43, Dietrich Bonhoeffer who was hanged by the Nazis at 39, Peter Marshall who died at 47, etc. Why would God invest such extraordinary ability in those whose lives would be abbreviated by death? I don't know.

On the other side of that question stand the individuals who were afforded long life despite their defiance of God. In 2 Kings 21, for example, we read of one such man. His name was Manasseh, son of the godly King Hezekiah. He was perhaps the most wicked despot ever to rule in Jerusalem. Manasseh came to power at 12 years of age, and "did evil in the eyes of the Lord" (v. 2) all the days of his life. He built altars to the false god Baal, even placing wooden idols in the temple of the Lord. He burned to death his own son, practiced witchcraft, consulted spiritists and mediums, and "did much evil in the eyes of the Lord, provoking him to anger" (v. 6). "Manasseh led them astray, so that they did more evil than the nations the Lord had destroyed before the Israelites" (v. 9). Finally, we read, "Manasseh also shed so much innocent blood that he filled Jerusalem from end to end—besides the sin that he had caused Judah to commit, so that they did evil in the eyes of the Lord" (v. 16). Because of this great wickedness, the judgment of God fell on subsequent generations—but not on Manasseh. He reigned 55 years and "rested with his fathers, and was buried in his palace garden, the garden of Uzza." End of story.

I have no doubt that terrible justice will be meted out to Manasseh on Judgment Day, but it does seem strange that he was permitted for 55 years to murder innocent people, sacrifice his children, and blaspheme the name of God. Uzzah, on the other hand, was killed instantly by God for a single misdeed—reaching out to steady the ark of the covenant lest it fall (2 Samuel 6:6-7). And in the New Testament, Ananias and Sapphira suffered the penalty of death for lying about their gifts to the body of believers (Acts 5:1-11). Something doesn't appear to add up here.

What conclusions can we draw from these seeming contradictions, except to "Let God be God"? He does not explain Himself to man. We *can* say with confidence that while His purposes and plans are very different from ours, He is infinitely just and His timing is always perfect. He intervenes at just the right moment for our ultimate good. Until we hear from Him, then, we would be wise not to get in a lather.

3. For reasons that are impossible to explain, we human beings are incredibly precious to God.

One of the most breathtaking concepts in all of Scripture is the revelation that God knows each of us personally and that we are in His mind both day and night. There is simply no way to comprehend the full implications of this love by the King of kings and Lord of lords. He is all-powerful and all-knowing, majestic and holy, from everlasting to everlasting. Why would He care about us—about our needs, our welfare, our fears? We have been discussing situations in which God doesn't make sense. His concern for us mere mortals is the most inexplicable of all.

Job also had difficulty understanding why the Creator would be interested in human beings. He asked, "What is man that you make so much of him, that you give him so much attention, that you examine him every morning . . . ?" (Job 7:17-18). David contemplated the same question when he wrote, "What is man that you are mindful of him, the son of man that you care for him?" (Psalm 8:4). And again in Psalm 139: "O Lord, you have searched me and you know me. You know when I sit and when I rise; you perceive my thoughts from afar. You discern my going out and my lying down; you are familiar with all my ways.

Before a word is on my tongue you know it completely, O Lord" (vv. 1-4). What an incredible concept!

Not only is the Lord "mindful" of each one of us, but He describes Himself throughout Scripture as our Father. In Luke 11:13 we read, "If you then, though you are evil, know how to give good gifts to your children, how much more will your Father in heaven give the Holy Spirit to those who ask him!" Psalm 103:13 says, "As a father has compassion on his children, so the Lord has compassion on those who fear him." But on the other hand, He is likened to a mother in Isaiah 66:13: "As a mother comforts her child, so will I comfort you."

Being a parent of two children, both now grown, I can identify with these parental analogies. They help me begin to comprehend how God feels about us. Shirley and I would give our lives for Danae and Ryan in a heartbeat if necessary. We pray for them every day, and they are never very far from our thoughts. And how vulnerable we are to their pain! Can it be that God actually loves His human family infinitely more than we, "being evil," can express to our own flesh and blood? That's what the Word teaches.

An incident occurred during our son's early childhood that illustrated for me this profound love of the heavenly Father. Ryan had a terrible ear infection when he was three years old that kept him (and us) awake most of the night. Shirley bundled up the toddler the next morning and took him to see the pediatrician. This doctor was an older man with very little patience for squirming kids. He wasn't overly fond of parents, either.

After examining Ryan, the doctor told Shirley that the infection had adhered itself to the eardrum and could only be treated by pulling the scab loose with a wicked little instrument. He warned that the procedure would hurt, and instructed Shirley to hold her son tightly on the table. Not only did this news alarm her, but enough of it was understood by Ryan to send him into orbit. It didn't take much to do that in those days.

Shirley did the best she could. She put Ryan on the examining table and attempted to hold him down. But he would have none of it. When the doctor inserted the pick-like instrument in his ear, the child broke loose and screamed to high heaven. The pediatrician then became angry at Shirley and told her if she couldn't follow instructions she'd have to go get her husband. I was in the neighborhood and quickly came to the examining room. After hearing what was needed, I swallowed hard and wrapped my 200-pound, 6-foot-2-inch frame around the toddler. It was one of the toughest moments in my career as a parent.

What made it so emotional was the horizontal mirror that Ryan was facing on the back side of the examining table. This made it possible for him to look directly at me as he screamed for mercy. I really believe I was in greater agony in that moment than my terrified little boy. It was too much. I turned him loose—and got a beefed-up version of the same bawling-out that Shirley had received a few minutes earlier. Finally, however, the grouchy pediatrician and I finished the task.

I reflected later on what I was feeling when Ryan was

going through so much suffering. What hurt me was the look on his face. Though he was screaming and couldn't speak, he was "talking" to me with those big blue eyes. He was saying, "Daddy! Why are you doing this to me? I thought you loved me. I never thought you would do anything like this! How could you . . . ? Please, please! Stop hurting me!"

It was impossible to explain to Ryan that his suffering was necessary for his own good, that I was trying to help him, that it was love that required me to hold him on the table. How could I tell him of my compassion in that moment? I would gladly have taken his place on the table, if possible. But in his immature mind, I was a traitor who had callously abandoned him.

Then I realized that there must be times when God also feels our intense pain and suffers along with us. Wouldn't that be characteristic of a Father whose love was infinite? How He must hurt when we say in confusion, "How could You do this terrible thing, Lord? Why me? I thought I could trust You! I thought You were my friend!" How can He explain within our human limitations that our agony is necessary, that it *does* have a purpose, that there are answers to the tragedies of life? I wonder if He anticipates the day when He can make us understand what was occurring in our time of trial. I wonder if He broods over our sorrows.

Some readers might doubt that an omnipotent God with no weaknesses and no needs is vulnerable to this kind of vicarious suffering. No one can be certain. We do know that Jesus experienced the broad range of human emotions, and then He told Philip, "Anyone who has seen me has seen the Father" (John 14:9). Remember that Jesus was "deeply moved in spirit and troubled" when Mary wept over Lazarus. He also wept as He looked over the city of Jerusalem and spoke of the sorrow that would soon come upon the Jewish people. Likewise, we are told that the Spirit intercedes for us now with "groans that words cannot express" (Romans 8:26). It seems logical to assume, therefore, that God, the Father, is passionately concerned about His human "family" and shares our grief in those unspeakable moments "when sorrows like sea billows roll." I believe He does.

4. Your arms are too short to box with God. Don't try it!

Several years ago, there was a Broadway theatrical performance called, "Your Arm's Too Short to Box with God." I didn't see it, but I agree with the premise behind the title. The human intellectual apparatus is pitifully ill-equipped to argue with the Creator. New Age followers don't agree. They say each of us can become gods in our own right by zoning in on a crystal and sitting cross-legged until our toes go to sleep. How presumptuous!

In a wonderful recorded sermon delivered by author Frank Peretti, he mocked the mumbo jumbo advice of New Agers on their journey to omnipotence. Frank asked us to picture Shirley MacLaine (who has in recent years become the High Priestess of the Weird) on a lonely beach somewhere. "Listen carefully, and you will hear her talking to the earth—or the moon—or somebody. She draws circles in the sand with her big toe and says in a squeaky voice, 'I . . . am god! I . . . am god!'" Sure you are, and I'm Julius Caesar.

No, we human beings hardly qualify as gods—even piddly ones. Despite our intense efforts to understand ourselves, we have learned very little about living together harmoniously or even what makes us tick. The best trained and most respected secular psychologists and psychiatrists still believe that man is basically good—that he only learns to do evil from society. If that were true, surely there would be at least one culture somewhere in the world where selfishness, dishonesty, and violence have not shown up. Instead, the history of human experience down through the millennia is the history of warfare—and murder and greed and exploitation. "Peace" is what we call that brief moment between wars when people stop to reload. And Plato said, "Only dead men have seen an end to war." He has been proved correct down across some 2,500 years. You might also take a good look at your children. How can anyone who has raised a toddler fail to recognize that rebellion, selfishness and aggression do not have to be cultivated. Kids come by it quite naturally. Thus, this most basic characteristic of human nature has been overlooked by those specifically trained to observe it.

Similar error riddles much of what we think and believe. Many scientific textbooks of 75 years ago seem like joke books today. Physicians in that era were still leeching people to "drain out the poisons." Even when I was in graduate school we were taught that humans had 48 chromosomes (the number is 46) and that Down's syndrome was caused by congenital influences (it is caused by one of several genetic anomalies). Certainly, we have learned much from the explosion of research and scientific investigation. I'm not disparaging that effort. I am saying that most of what was believed in ages past was palpably wrong. Could it be that we are living today in the first period in human history when nearly everything we have concluded is accurate? No chance!

This is the point made earlier: If human intelligence and perception are undependable in assessing everyday reality, which can be seen, touched, heard, tasted, and smelled, how much less capable is it of evaluating the unfathomable God of the universe? Our efforts to encapsulate and comprehend Him are equally as futile. We can only delve so far into the infinite mind of the Maker before we run out of marbles. Still, the arrogance of mankind in ignoring or challenging the wisdom of the Almighty is shocking at times.

A story is told about the British general Bernard (Monty) Montgomery, who had a notoriously large ego. He was giving a speech one day in which he related a conversation between Moses and God. Montgomery said, "As God pointed out to Moses—and I think rightly so—" I'm sure the Lord was relieved to hear that Monty approved of His advice to Moses. Other examples of man's arrogance are not so humorous, such as the notion that the genius of creation simply evolved over time, with no design and no Designer. The Lord must marvel at the stupidity of that idea. I've also wondered how He feels about the U.S. Supreme Court's ruling that the Ten Commandments cannot be posted on a public school bulletin board.

Job tried to question God and was given a rather pointed history lesson in response. Note especially the first sentence from the mouth of the Lord.

> *Who is this that darkens my counsel with words without knowledge? Brace yourself like a man; I will question you, and you shall answer me. Where were you when I laid the earth's foundation? Tell me, if you understand. Who marked off its dimensions? Surely you know! Who stretched a measuring line across it? On what were its footings set, or who laid its cornerstone—while the morning stars sang together and all the angels shouted for joy? (Job 38:2-7)*

God continued that discourse until Job got his mind straight, and then the Lord added these words, "Will the one who contends with the Almighty correct him? Let him who accuses God answer him!" (Job 40:2). Job got the message. He replied, "I am unworthy—how can I reply to you? I put my hand over my mouth. I spoke once, but I have no answer—twice, but I will say no more" (Job 40:4-5).

There have been a few times in my life when I've made the same mistake as Job, demanding answers from God. One such occasion is a source of embarrassment to me today. It is too personal to relate in detail, except to say there was something I wanted the Lord to do for me that I thought I needed very badly. It seemed in keeping with His Word, and I set out to assure that my prayer was answered. I prayed every day for weeks, begging God to grant this request that seemed to be so significant. I was literally on my face before Him during this time of petition. Nevertheless, He clearly said no! He didn't explain or apologize. He simply shut the door. At first I was hurt, and then I became angry. I knew better, but I was tempted to say with sarcasm, "Would it have been too troublesome for You to have taken a moment from Your busy day to hear the cry of your servant?" I did not utter these words, but I couldn't help what I felt. And I felt abandoned.

Well, two years went by and my circumstances changed radically. The matter that I had prayed about began to look very different. Ultimately I realized that it would have been most unfortunate if the Lord had granted my request in that instance. He loved me enough to turn me down, even when I was demanding my own way.

Others have also lived to regret what they had asked for. I knew a teenage girl who fell madly in love with an adolescent Romeo and pleaded with God to turn his heart in her direction. The petition was flatly denied. Thirty-five years later when their paths crossed again, she was shocked to see that the gorgeous hunk of masculinity she remembered had turned into an unmotivated, paunchy, middle-aged bore. She recalled her youthful prayer and whispered ever so quietly, *"Thank you, Lord!"*

Admittedly, most of our spiritual frustrations do not end with an enlightened, "Oh, now I see what You were doing, Lord!" We just have to file them under the heading, "Things I Don't Understand," and leave it there. In those instances, we should be thankful that He does what is best for us whether or not it contradicts our wishes. Even a reasonably good parent sometimes says "no" to a child's demands.

I've been trying to say with this discussion that our view of God is too small—that His power and His wisdom cannot even be imagined by us mortals. He is not just "the man upstairs" or "the great chauffeur in the sky," or some kind of Wizard who will do a dance for those who make the right noises. We dare not trivialize the One about whom it is written,

> *Praise be to you, O Lord, God of our father Israel, from everlasting to everlasting. Yours, O Lord, is the greatness and the power and the glory and the majesty and the splendor, for everything in heaven and earth is yours. Yours, O Lord, is the kingdom; you are exalted as head over all. Wealth and honor come from you; you are the ruler of all things. In your hands are strength and power to exalt and give strength to all. Now, our God, we give you thanks, and praise your glorious name. (1 Chronicles 29:10-13)*

If we truly understood the majesty of this Lord and the depth of His love for us, we would certainly accept those times when He defies human logic and sensibilities. Indeed, that is what we *must* do. Expect confusing experiences to occur along the way. Welcome them as friends—as opportunities for your faith to grow. Hold fast to your faith, without which it is impossible to please Him. Never let yourself succumb to the "betrayal barrier," which is Satan's most effective tool against us. Instead, store away your questions for a lengthy conversation on the other side, and then press on toward the mark. Any other approach is foolhardy—because your arms are too short to box with God.

4

ACCEPTANCE
OR
DESPAIR

Perhaps the most dramatic example of our theme occurred in the life of the great patriarch, Abraham, more than 4,000 years ago. Our interest in his story focuses on the barrenness of his wife, Sarah. She remained infertile throughout her childbearing years, causing continual grief and embarrassment. But when Abraham was 75 years old, he began receiving promises from God that he would become the father of a great nation, and that in him, all the nations of the world would be blessed (Genesis 12:2-3). That was wonderful news for a man with no heir and a woman who ached to be a mother.

What followed that promise, however, was a long period of silence on the subject. Finally, the Lord visited Abraham again. He said, "All the land that you see I will give to you and your offspring forever. I will make your offspring like the dust of the earth, so that if anyone could count the dust, then your offspring could be counted" (Genesis 13:15-16).

These were strange words spoken to a man whose wife had tried to have a baby for perhaps 40 years. Yet Abraham accepted the promise—and waited patiently for its fulfillment. But no child came. Years passed before the Lord reassured His servant for the third time. On this occasion, however, Abraham revealed his growing confusion on the matter by replying, "O Sovereign Lord, what can you give me since I remain childless?" (Genesis 15:2).

It was a valid question from the aging Abraham. The Lord responded by taking him out under the night sky and saying, "'Look up at the heavens and count the stars—if indeed you can count them.' Then he said to him, 'So shall your offspring be'" (Genesis 15:5).

These promises of blessing were followed by Sarah's continued infertility and yet another period of silence. What Abraham faced at this point was a classic case of "God contradicting God." The Lord did not honor His word or explain His delay. The facts didn't add up. The pieces didn't fit. Sarah had gone through menopause, effectively ending her hope of motherhood. By then, she and her husband were old, and we can assume that their sexual passion had diminished. Despite these improbabilities, however, Scripture tells us Abraham "believed the Lord, and he credited it to him as righteousness" (Genesis 15:6).

The rest of the account is one of the most familiar and beloved stories in the Bible. Sarah did, indeed, become pregnant when she was 90 years of age and Abraham was 100. Soon a son was born and he was named Isaac (meaning "laughter"). What a joyful moment it was for them. God had performed a mighty miracle just as He promised, and Abraham was given an heir. However, the drama wasn't over for these new but very old parents.

Some years later when Isaac had become a young man, there occurred one of the most confusing events in biblical history. God told Abraham to sacrifice the son who had been so long anticipated! What a strange and distressing message! How could the old patriarch have begun to understand what the Lord was doing? Wasn't Isaac the key to the breathtaking promises of God? If Isaac was to be sacrificed, from whom would come millions of descendants, the many kings (including the Messiah), a mighty nation through which the world would be blessed, everlasting possession of the Promised Land, and a perpetual covenant with Jehovah? All of these prophecies depended specifically on Isaac, who was soon to die.

But that was only the way things seemed through human senses. In truth, the promises given to Abraham did not depend on Isaac at all. They depended entirely on God. He is never boxed in by human limitations. And God had everything under perfect control. A divinely appointed plan was unfolding that would bear meaning for all mankind. Isaac's miraculous birth was symbolic of the coming Christ child. The command to sacrifice Isaac on the altar pointed toward "the Lamb that was slain from the creation of the world" (Revelation 13:8). When Isaac carried the wood to be used for the fire which would burn his body, he foretold the time 2,000 years hence when Jesus carried His own cross to Golgotha. Isaac's willingness to be killed by his aged father was symbolic of the Messiah's submission to His Father and to His executioners. Some theologians even believe Isaac's sacrifice was to have occurred on the exact site of Jesus' crucifixion. Every component of the story had prophetic significance. Of course, Abraham understood nothing of the plan. Given his confusion and what was at stake for him, it is amazing that this godly man would have obediently carried out Isaac's sacrifice if an angel hadn't intervened.

One of my favorite Scriptures summarizes this episode from the perspective of New Testament times. This is how the Apostle Paul described Abraham nearly 2000 years later:

> *Without weakening in his faith, he faced the fact that his body was as good as dead—since he was about a hundred years old—and that Sarah's womb was also dead. Yet he did not waver through unbelief regarding the promise of God, but was strengthened in his faith and gave glory to God, being fully persuaded that God had power to do what he had promised. This is why "it was credited to him as righteousness." (Romans 4:19-22)*

In other words, Abraham believed God even when God didn't make sense. The facts clearly said, "It is impossible for this thing to happen." The Lord had made "empty promises" for nearly 25 years, and still there was no sign of action. Unanswered questions and troubling contradictions swirled through the air. Nevertheless, Abraham "did not waver through unbelief." Why? Because he was convinced that God could transcend reason and factual evidence. And this is why he is called the "father of our faith."

Well, so much for Abraham and his wife Sarah. What about you and me and the times in which we live? Is there a lesson for mankind in this historical event? There certainly is! A moment will also come in your lifetime when the facts will lead to despair. Maybe that moment has already arrived. At those times God seems to contradict Himself and no satisfactory explanation is forthcoming. The particular nature of the confusion varies from person to person, but a crisis of some dimension is inevitable. Faith never goes unchallenged for long. The question is, How will we deal with it when it comes? Will we break and run? Will we waver in disbelief? Will we "curse God and die," as Job's wife suggested? I pray not! And if we prepare now for the experience, I believe we can steel ourselves against the assault of that hour.

My friend Robert Vernon recently had to deal with his own version of that universal crisis. Bob is the former assistant chief of police, Los Angeles Police Department, where he served with distinction for 37 years. Toward the end of his tenure, however, he was unjustly and illegally pressured to resign because of his conservative Christian beliefs. After many unsuccessful attempts by the media to discredit him in the police department, Chief Vernon's critics began looking at his private life for something with which to embarrass him. They soon found it. Someone dug up a cassette recording of a speech Bob had delivered at his church 14 years earlier. On the basis of comments he made about family life, taken out of context and wildly distorted, they forced an investigation of Vernon's work at the police department. It was a clear violation of his First Amendment rights. Since when can a person be persecuted for expressing his religious views in his own church? That question is being considered now by the courts, but there is clear evidence of bias there, too.

Please understand, there was never *any* accusation of professional malfeasance against Chief Vernon in any official capacity. Nevertheless, a full-scale investigation was conducted to see if his religious views might have affected his work. He was eventually cleared of all wrongdoing, although his leadership was so damaged by the inquisition that he felt it necessary to resign. I know Chief Vernon personally, and I can say with certainty that he was hounded out of office simply because of his faith, despite his 37 years of unblemished service.

Chief Vernon's experience offers us an opportunity to examine a classic case of "faith under fire." His situation bears all the typical components: a very troubling event, an element of injustice or unfairness (Why me?), a silent God who could have intervened but didn't, and a million unanswered questions. Have you ever been there?

Bob was asked to speak at a recent chapel service for the employees of Focus on the Family, and he elected to discuss his own difficulties. I think you'll find his remarks helpful, especially if you're enduring your own private trial at this time. This is what the veteran policeman said to our staff:

> When it became apparent that Daryl Gates would soon resign as Chief of Police, an article appeared in a Los Angeles magazine. It said, "Those who are anxious to get rid of Gates ought to see who's standing in the wings to take his place. It's one Robert L. Vernon, who has very strange religious beliefs." Then they listed three things that I had reportedly said in a speech recorded 14 years earlier. I stand by what I actually said, and I'm not apologizing for it. Those concepts came from the Word of God. But the magazine perverted my actual comments and said, "First, he believes homosexuality is a sin." That's true. Second, they said, "He believes that women should submit to men." That's not true. I referred to what the Bible says about mutual submission in husband-wife relationships. Third, my critics twisted what I had said about child discipline. I was talking about a father who had not kept his promise to his son and provoked the boy to wrath. When the child became rebellious, the father said, "If you have a rebel on your hands, you have to break him—and to break him you have to beat him." I was quoting the father, not speaking for myself. I went on to say, "Who was wrong in this scenario? The father was at fault, not the son."
>
> The magazine, however, ascribed the father's words to me, and then concluded, "Here's what Chief Vernon thinks about raising children." They

edited the tape in such a way that the listener heard only my voice recommending that we beat children until they break. That edited tape was given to the news media, which released it widely. It was a very clever maneuver.

As a result, my reputation was severely damaged. I eventually had to leave the Los Angeles Police Department and have not been able to get a job in police work elsewhere. I recently applied for a position north of Denver, but they didn't even interview me. I am, you see, a religious kook. I believe weird things. I now know what Solomon meant when he said, "A good name is better than gold and silver, yea, precious stones."

I even have Christian friends who have heard my recording on the radio and said, "We know you denied it, Bob, but we heard you say that children should be beaten until they break." I try to explain, but sometimes it's hard to make them understand. I have to confess something to you. I not only got depressed about this situation, but I also became angry at God. And that wasn't right.

About that time I had an experience that helped clarify some things for me. My son and I decided to float down the Colorado River on a raft. It was a dramatic ride, I can assure you. We left with 18 friends from a place called Lee's Ferry. As we floated out for the eight-day journey, someone said, "Well, we're committed." We sure were. By the third day there were some who had had enough. But that *was too bad. There was no way out of the canyon except down the river. That's the way the Lord works when we're faced with a time of difficulty. Don't think about ways to squirm out of trouble. Just stay committed and you'll come through in due course.*

There were some extremely turbulent places along the path of the river. At Lava Falls, for example, the raft dropped 37 vertical feet in a distance of 75 feet. Our raft-master, named Robin, would say as we approached such a place, "This is gonna be a good one." By that he meant, "We're all gonna die!" Finally, we came to Kermit Falls, which for us was the most violent spot in the river. Suddenly, Robin seemed to lose control of the raft just as we started down the rapids. It spun sideways at the worst possible moment. For an instant, I was tempted to jump overboard. I really thought we were going to die. Then I heard the big Evinrude engine roaring at peak performance behind the raft. I realized that Robin had turned sideways on purpose. Then I saw a huge, jagged rock that had tumbled down from the walls of that great canyon. It was sticking up menacingly in the center of the river. That's why Robin spun the craft. He did it so the full power of the motor could push us around the dangerous rock. If I had jumped from the raft, I'd have drowned or would have been crushed on the jagged rock.

To those of you who are plunging over the falls today, resist the temptation to jump overboard! God knows what He is doing. He has your raft sideways for a reason. Even though your reputation may have been ruined, you're depressed, and you're wondering what to do next. If you'll listen carefully, you'll hear the One who said to David, "Trust in Me!"

From my experience on the river, and from reading Psalm 37, I've learned not to fret. I've confessed my anger to him and said, "You know what You're doing even though my raft seems out of control. I will trust you. I delight in You. I've committed my way unto You. Now, I'm 'resting' in my circumstances." But then, I had to learn the most difficult lesson of all. As my wife and I read the other Psalms, one word kept jumping out at us. It was the word, "wait."

"No, Lord! I don't want to wait. I want relief today. Please take revenge on those who have hurt me." But He says, "Be still and know that I am God." Then He led me to the final four verses in Psalm 37, which tell us:

"Consider the blameless, observe the upright; there is a future for the man of peace. But all sinners will be destroyed; the future of the wicked will be cut off. The salvation of the righteous comes from the Lord; he is their stronghold in time of trouble. The Lord helps them and delivers them; he delivers them from the wicked and saves them, because they take refuge in him" (Psalm 37:37-40). [1]

---

1 You can read Bob Vernon's story in greater detail in his book: Robert L. Vernon, *L.A. Justice* (Colorado Springs: Focus on the Family, 1993).

Those words from Chief Vernon reflect great maturity and faith, considering the injustice and pain he and his wife, Esther, have suffered. I have shared his message here because so many of my readers have experienced similar difficulties. Are you one of them? Is your raft skidding sideways in the river today? Is it plunging down the rapids towards the rocks below, terrifying everyone on board? Have you considered jumping into the river and trying to swim to safety on your own? That is precisely what Satan would have you do. He wants you to give up on God, who seems to have lost control of your circumstances. But I urge you not to leave the safety of His protection. The Captain knows what He is doing. There are purposes that you cannot perceive or comprehend. You may never understand—at least not in this life—but you must not let go of your faith. It is, after all, "the evidence of things *not* seen" (Hebrews 11:1, KJV).

Before pressing on, there is another example of "faith under fire" that I think is worth considering. It occurred in the family of Dr. Jim and Sally Conway and will represent the experience of millions around the world. Whereas Chief Vernon struggled with injustice and professional embarrassment, the Conways dealt with an even more serious problem. The life of their precious daughter was threatened. I'll let Dr. Conway tell his own story, as heard on the Focus on the Family radio broadcast:

> *When our daughter was 15 years of age, she began having trouble with one of her knees. For a year*

and one-half, she saw doctors, had laboratory tests and scans, and two extensive biopsies on the tumor they found. We waited for weeks for word from the many pathology labs around the United States who were studying her mysterious lump. Finally one evening our physician came to our house and gave some very distressing news. He said that Becki had a malignancy, and that it was necessary to amputate her leg. You can imagine how that devastated Sally and me. I refused to believe it. I determined to prevent this surgery by praying until God promised to heal her.

"You're not going to have your leg amputated," I told Becki. "I believe God is going to do a miracle. He said we could come to Him in times of trouble. I'm absolutely convinced you are going to be spared this surgery."

Our church then began a 24-hour vigil of fasting and prayer. Thousands of people around the United States and overseas were praying for Becki's healing.

On the morning when the surgery was scheduled, I said to our physician, "Scott, as you go into the operating room, please verify that the cancer has been healed. God is going to come through. I'm sure."

He left and did not immediately return. Forty-five minutes went by, and still, Sally, my other two daughters, and I sat in the waiting room. An hour passed, and then two. I began to realize that a lengthy medical procedure must be in progress. Then the doctor came out and told me that they had amputated Becki's leg. I was absolutely shattered. I was crushed. I lost God! In anger, I was beating on the walls of the hospital and saying, "Where are You, God? Where are You?"

I was in a state of shock and wandered down to the morgue in the basement of the hospital. That's where I felt I belonged, surrounded by death. I was dealing with more than Becki's surgery, as terrible as that was. I struggled to handle the theological implications of what had happened. I could not understand why God permitted this to happen. You see, if I had been a plumber instead of a pastor, I could have gone out to fix pipes the next day, and my spiritual confusion would not have affected my work. But my job required me to stand before people and teach them the principles of the Bible. What could I tell them now?

If I had been a liberal pastor who didn't believe the Bible to be literally true, I could have survived by doing book reviews and talking about irrelevant stuff. But I pastored a Bible church. My style of teaching was exposition of the Word, reviewing it verse by verse and drawing out its meaning. How could I go back and tell my people that God had let my daughter lose her leg? It was a terrible moment in my life.

As I sat outside the morgue that day, a friend found me in the bowels of the hospital and came to my rescue. He was a Godsend to me! I'm not part of the Charismatic movement, but it was Dick Foth, an

Assembly of God pastor, who stood by my side and cried with me and prayed for me. He said, "I'm not worried about Becki. I'm worried about you. There are a couple of thousand people in your church and thousands more elsewhere who are hanging on for you. You're going to get through this." Then he and two other guys took turns working with me. One would go for a coffee break and the others would take over. They just kept me talking—letting me spill out the frustration and the anger.

They didn't condemn me even though I was so angry at God. At one point I said, "I think He was so busy finding a parking spot for a little old lady that He didn't have time to save Becki's leg." Dick would listen and then say, "Is there anything else you need to say?" I didn't have to worry that if I said something disturbing, maybe these guys would doubt God. I didn't worry about them giving up on me. I didn't have to hold anything in and say, "I've got to keep up the professional front because I'm a preacher. I've got to be good." They let me deal with the pain.

When a person is going through this kind of terrible depression, some believers don't know how to respond. They say, "I'll pray for you," which may mean, "I'm no longer really listening to you." That can be a way of ending one's responsibility to shoulder the load. In fact, when it comes to bearing one another's burdens, the secular world sometimes does that job better than we do. They know the importance of letting resent-

ment and anger spill out, whereas Christians may feel they have to hold it inside. The Scripture tells us, "The righteous cry out, and the Lord hears them; he delivers them from all their troubles" (Psalm 34:17).

It also bothered me later when people began offering simplistic explanations and flippant comments to "cheer me up." It was irritating when they quoted Romans 8:28, "all things work together for good," when they had not earned the right to brush off my pain. I wanted to say, "Tell me about it, Charlie. Tell me about it when your 16-year-old daughter's leg is amputated. Come back when you've gone through something like this, and then we'll talk again." Sometimes we get so used to the "cheer-up" mode in Christianity that we become unreal. I almost heard people saying to me in those days, "Shhhhh! Don't say those things. What if God hears them?"

As if God didn't know what I was thinking and struggling with! God knew what I was going through, and He understood my passion. My love for Becki originated with Him in the first place. So who would I be trying to fool by covering up the agony of my soul?

I remember a guy I saw in a restaurant a few days after Becki underwent surgery. He was sitting at a table, and as I walked by he reached out and grabbed my coat. He said, "Jim, I think God has allowed this to happen because it has brought about a revival in our church."

I said, "So what is God going to do to bring another revival when this one passes, chop off Becki's other leg? Then her arm and her other arm? There isn't enough of Becki to keep any church spiritually alive, if that is what it takes."

When you start reaching for puny answers like that, it dehumanizes those who suffer and insults our magnificent God who loves and cares for the oppressed. I couldn't explain why Becki had to lose her leg, but I knew the answers being given were not right.

Probably the most important thing I learned in this entire process is this: I became deeply aware that there were only two choices that I could make. One was to continue in my anger at God and follow the path of despair I was on. The other choice was to let God be God, and somehow say, "I don't know how all this fits together. I don't understand the reasons for it. I'm not even going to ask for the explanation. I've chosen to accept the fact that You are God and I'm the servant, instead of the other way around." And there I left it.

It was in that choice that I came to cope with my situation. I frankly admit that after all these years, I still struggle with some things. I still get sick to my stomach when I see my daughter hopping on one leg. But I have come to recognize that God has a higher purpose and I just don't understand that purpose. I am prepared to wait until eternity to receive answers to my questions, if necessary. Like Job, I am now able to say, "Though he *slay me, yet will I trust in him" (Job 13:15, KJV). It's either despair, or it's the acceptance of His sovereignty. Those are the alternatives.*

Let me say it again. It's either despair, or it's God. There's nothing in between. Our family has chosen to hold on to God.[2]

Thank you, Dr. Jim Conway, and your wife Sally and daughter Becki, for letting us share your deepest pain. Seldom in the Christian community have we witnessed such honesty and vulnerability. I trust that God will continue to use your experience to strengthen the faith of those who sit alone today, symbolically, in the morgue. All they have believed and hoped has been assaulted by the forces of hell. The philosophical and theological foundation on which everything rests has just given way. So what do they do now?

There is only one answer, and it is the conclusion drawn by Dr. Jim Conway in his hour of crisis: Don't demand explanations. Don't lean on your ability to understand. Don't turn loose of your faith. But do choose to trust Him, by the exercise of the will He has placed within you. The only other alternative—is despair.

---

2 You can read Jim, Sally, and Becki's story in greater detail in their book, Becki Conway Sanders and Jim & Sally Conway, *Trusting God in a Family Crisis* (Downers Grove, Ill.: InterVarsity Press, 1989).

5

"HE WILL DELIVER US, BUT IF NOT . . ."

We must hasten now to deal with a series of questions that are critical to everything we have discussed to this point: What is God's role in situations that confuse and sometimes disillusion His followers? Where was He amidst the challenges that confronted Chief Bob and Esther Vernon, Dr. Jim and Sally Conway, Darryl and Clarita Gustafson, Dr. Jerry and Mary White, Drs. Chuck and Karen Frye, and the others we have considered? Specifically, does God hear and answer the prayers of His people?

A surprisingly large percentage of Americans believe deeply in the efficacy of prayer. In a *Newsweek* cover story entitled "Talking to God" (January 6, 1992), the Gallup Poll reported that 78 percent of Americans prayed once a week and 57 percent prayed at least once per day. Ninety-one percent of women prayed at some time and 85 percent of men. This included 94 percent of blacks and 87 percent of whites.

"Some of these prayers," Newsweek commented, "are born *in extremis:* there are few atheists in cancer wards or unemployment lines. But in allegedly rootless, materialistic, self-centered America, there is also a hunger for a personal experience with God that prayer seeks to satisfy."

The authors concluded:

Even in the university, the temple of all that the Enlightenment has distilled, prayer has found a home. "It was very rare 20 years ago to find vital, vibrant religion on the college campus," says David Rosenhan, professor of law and psychology at Stanford University. "Now there are prayer meetings here that are attended by 300 to 500 students regularly."

I'm not naive enough to believe that all these praying Americans were seeking a committed relationship with the Living God. For some, prayer is only an inch or two from superstition, such as astrology or any other shot in the dark. Nevertheless, the receptivity for things of the Spirit is very encouraging to those of us who have longed for a revival of religious fervor in the nation.

But what do *you* believe about the meaning of prayer? Is it true, as James 5:16 says, that "the prayer of a righteous man is powerful and effective"? Was Jesus speaking to us when He said, "Ask and it will be given to you; seek and you will find; knock and the door will be opened to you" (Matthew 7:7)?

Speaking personally, I have staked my life on the validity of those promises. They were "God-breathed" and then dutifully recorded by the inspired writers of the Word. Our foundation as believers is rooted in the Scriptures, where the message is unmistakable. Consider these verses:

Look to the Lord and his strength; seek his face always. (1 Chronicles 16:11)

The Lord detests the sacrifice of the wicked, but the prayer of the upright pleases him. (Proverbs 15:8)

Then Jesus told his disciples a parable to show them that they should always pray and not give up. (Luke 18:1)

In the same way, the Spirit helps us in our weakness. We do not know what we ought to pray for, but the Spirit himself intercedes for us with groans that words cannot express. (Romans 8:26)

Do not be anxious about anything, but in everything, by prayer and petition, with thanksgiving, present your requests to God. (Philippians 4:6)

Devote yourself to prayer, being watchful and thankful. (Colossians 4:2)

Pray continually; give thanks in all circumstances, for this is God's will for you in Christ Jesus. (1 Thessalonians 5:17-18)

I want men everywhere to lift up holy hands in prayer, without anger or disputing. (1 Timothy 2:8)

It is obvious not only that prayer is honored by the Lord, but that we are *commanded* to enter into this personal communication with Him. And what a privilege it is! Have you considered the nature of this gift we have been granted by the Almighty? We need not make an appointment to get His attention. There are no administrative assistants or secretaries with whom we must negotiate. He never puts us off to a later date when His schedule is less congested.

Instead, we are invited to walk boldly into His presence at any moment, day or night. He hears the faintest cry of the sick, the lonely, the despised of the world. Every one of us is known and loved by Him, despite our imperfection and failures. Truly, the invitation to prayer is a precious expression of the Creator's incomparable love and compassion for humanity. That understanding has been woven into the fabric of my life and family from earliest childhood.

The year was 1957, and I was a senior in college. An ominous telephone call came one afternoon from my parents, who sounded anxious and upset. Mom quickly told me that my dad had developed an angry-looking sore on his right hand. They had watched it for some time and realized it was not healing. Finally they went to see a dermatologist and had just returned from his office. My father, age 46, was diagnosed as having carcinoma, squamous cell—a type of skin cancer that is curable in the early stages but dangerous if not treated. The doctor seemed concerned. He told them that a microscopic examination of tissue revealed a "very mature" cell. He couldn't tell whether or not it had metastasized (spread to other parts of the body), but he could not rule out that possibility.

It was decided to treat the cancer with radiation over a period of six weeks. At the end of that time, the healing process should begin. If the lesion was controllable locally, it would disappear entirely in about five more weeks. But if it did not heal, more serious problems were ahead. The specter of amputation was raised. My father was an artist, and the thought of losing his right arm (or his life) alarmed the entire family. We began praying for him.

Four weeks after completing the radiation treatments, the sore was still much the same. No sign of healing had occurred. Tension mounted as we continued to get discouraging medical reports. (I'm sure the disease would be less challenging today than in the fifties, but the episode was extremely distressing at that time.) My father's physician began contemplating the next step.

It was time to do some more intensive praying. Dad went to our denominational leaders and requested that they anoint him with oil and specifically ask the Lord to heal the cancer. That brief service occurred two days before the end of the fifth week, at which point the dermatologist had indicated a further decision would have to be made. Exactly two days later, the sore healed over. It never returned.

This is but one example of dramatic answers to prayer that I witnessed during my childhood and youth. Illustrations from that era could fill this book, quite literally, because we were a family that believed in prayer. So many stories come to mind. I remember an occasion when my father had given his entire paycheck to a pastor whose children needed shoes and warm clothes. Dad was a soft touch for anyone with a financial problem. Inevitably, we ran out of money a few days later—and went straight to our knees. I can still hear my father praying after he had gathered his little family around.

He said, "Now Lord, You said if we would honor You in our good times that You would be faithful to us in times of need. And as You know, we could use a little help to get us through."

I tell you honestly that a check for $1,200 came in the mail the day following that prayer. My faith grew by leaps and bounds during those formative years, because I saw God responding to a family that depended upon Him. It happened hundreds of times.

My wife, Shirley, did not grow up in a Christian home, and her experiences were very different from mine. Her father was an alcoholic who abused his family and spoke of God only when cursing. Shirley's mother, while not a Christian, was a wonderful woman who loved her two children. She recognized her need for assistance in raising her kids and began sending them to a neighborhood evangelical church when they were very young. There, Shirley learned about Jesus— and she learned to pray.

This little girl, trapped in poverty and the heartache of alcoholism, began talking to the Lord about her family. Especially after her parents were divorced, she asked Him to grant two requests. First, she prayed for a Christian stepfather who would love and provide for them. Second, Shirley knew she wanted to have a godly home and family someday. She began asking the Lord for a Christian husband when the time came to marry. It touches my heart today to think about that child, alone on her knees in her bedroom, talking to God about her need. I was out there somewhere oblivious of her existence, but the Lord had me in a long-term training program. By the time I met this pretty young lady in college, I did not have to be pushed.

That story beautifully illustrates the efficacy of prayer. The great God of the universe, with all His majesty and power, was not too busy to hear the small voice of a child in need. He not only brought the two of us together, but He sent a fine, never-married man to be Shirley's new stepfather. Both her parents are Christians today and are serving the Lord in their community.

When Shirley and I met and fell in love, therefore, we each brought a strong faith to the relationship. From those early days, we determined that Jesus Christ would have the preeminent place in our lives. I remember the two of us sitting in my junky old Mercury before we were married and expressing a prayer of dedication for our future home. We asked the Lord to direct our paths, and especially, to put His blessing on any children He might loan to us. Then I pledged to Shirley that I would spend the rest of my life trying to provide the kind of happiness and security she had missed as a child. This was the foundation on which our little family was built.

Now, after more than three decades together, we have seen God's consistent faithfulness in response to our prayers. I don't know where we would be without this source of strength and sustenance. In fact, the most significant development of our marriage has been the growth and maturation of Shirley's prayer life. She has become what is sometimes called a "prayer warrior," maintaining a constant communion with the Lord. It is fitting, given this spiritual fervor, that she has been appointed chairman of the National Day of Prayer.

Now let me wade into deeper water. Although hundreds of Scriptures tell us that God hears and answers prayer, it is important to acknowledge what most of us have already observed—that He does not do everything we ask in the manner that we would desire. Years may pass before we see the fulfillment of His purposes. There are other occasions when He says "no," or "wait." And let's be honest, there are times when He says nothing at all. As we have indicated, many believers become confused and wounded in those instances, and their faith begins to wobble.

This disillusionment was the theme of a classic novel by W. Somerset Maugham entitled *Of Human Bondage*. The principal character was a young man with a clubfoot who had hated his deformity from earliest childhood. When he discovered Christianity, he thought he had found a quick way to get rid of it. He began praying that God would heal his foot and make him normal. As it became apparent that his repeated requests would not be granted, he felt his faith had been invalidated, and he lost interest in God. I wonder how many times that unfortunate drama has been reenacted through the centuries.

Every long-term believer has had the experience of praying for something that God appeared not to grant. As a case in point, let's return to the story of my father's skin cancer. Although he was healed of this disease, both he and my mother are in heaven today. Our prayers regarding subsequent illnesses did not keep them earthbound when the Lord called them across the Great Divide. If that is troubling to the reader, remember that Lazarus, whom Jesus miraculously raised from the dead, later died again. *Every* person Jesus healed eventually passed away. It is said that time heals all wounds. That may be true, but it also wounds all heals.

Does this seem contradictory to the affirmation of prayer I have expressed? It shouldn't! Consider for a moment the kind of world it would be if God did exactly what we demanded in every instance. First, believers would outlive nonbelievers by centuries. The rest of the human family would be trapped in decaying bodies, but Christians and their children would live in an idyllic world set apart. They would never have toothaches or kidney stones or myopic vision. All of their businesses would succeed and their homes would be beautiful, etc. The entire basis for the God-man relationship would be undermined. People would seek a friendship with Him in order to gain the fringe benefits, rather than responding with a heart of repentance and love. Indeed, the most greedy among us would be the first to be drawn to the benefits of the

Christian life. Most importantly, these evidences of God's awesome power would eliminate the need for faith. As Paul wrote in Romans 8:24, "Hope that is seen is no hope at all. Who hopes for what he already has?"

Our faith, then, is anchored not in signs and wonders but in the sovereign God of the universe. He will not "perform" on cue to impress us. Jesus condemned those who wanted Him to put His miracles on display, saying, "A wicked and adulterous generation asks for a miraculous sign! But none will be given it" (Matthew 12:39). He wants us to accept Him in the absence of proof. Jesus told Thomas, "Blessed are those who have not seen and yet have believed" (John 20:29). We serve this Lord not because He dances to our tune, but because we trust His preeminence in our lives. Ultimately, He must be—He *will* be—the determiner of what is in our best interest. We can't see the future. We don't know His plan. We perceive only the small picture, and not even that very clearly. Given this limitation, it seems incredibly arrogant to tell God what to do—rather than making our needs known and then yielding to His divine purposes.

Jesus Himself modeled that attitude of submission for us. He asked His Father in the Garden of Gethsemane that the "cup" of humiliation and death be removed from Him. He knew fully what the crucifixion meant. The emotional pressure was so intense that great drops of blood penetrated His skin. Medically speaking, that phenomenon is called hematidrosis, and it occurs only in persons undergoing the most severe distress. Yet even in the midst of that agony, Jesus prayed, "Yet not my will, but yours be done" (Luke 22:42).

There are many other biblical examples of this yielding to divine authority. The Apostle Paul asked the Lord on three separate occasions to remove the irritant he called "a thorn in the flesh." Three times the answer was no. Instead, he was told, "My grace is sufficient for you, for my power is made perfect in weakness" (2 Corinthians 12:9).

You'll also remember the story of Moses and his encounter with the voice of God in the burning bush (Exodus 3–4). The Lord instructed him to confront Pharaoh and demand that the children of Israel be released from Egyptian captivity. When Moses asked why the children of Israel should believe God had sent him, the Lord armed him with miraculous powers. He turned his staff into a snake and back again into a staff. Then He caused Moses' hand to become leprous and made it healthy again. Finally, God told him that if they would not believe those two signs, he should take water from the Nile River and pour it on the ground and it would turn into blood. These startling feats were designed to reveal the power of God and to authenticate Moses as His representative.

But then a curious thing happened. Moses complained that he lacked eloquence for the task—"I am slow of speech and tongue" (Exodus 4:10)—yet the Lord did not offer to heal that infirmity. Doesn't that seem strange? He had just performed uncanny miracles that enabled Moses to carry out His mission. Why

wouldn't He eliminate this troublesome speech imped-
iment? He certainly had the power to do so. Wouldn't
it have been logical for the Lord to have said, "You're
going to need a strong voice to lead a million people
through the wilderness. Henceforth, you will speak
with authority!" No, that isn't the way Jehovah responded. First, He became angry at Moses for using this
source of weakness as an excuse. Then He designated
Aaron, Moses' brother, to serve as his mouthpiece. Why
didn't He just "do the job right" and get rid of the
problem? We don't know. As I've said before, there are
times when God doesn't make sense.

We can assume that the Lord didn't heal Moses'
"slowness of tongue" because Moses, like Paul, was
learning that his strength was made perfect in weakness. He was chosen for leadership not because he was
a miracle-worker or a superman but because the Lord
determined to use his inadequacies and shortcomings.

Thank God, I was accepted under the same provision.
Each of us is riddled with flaws and shortcomings that the
Lord could overcome with a whisper. Instead, He often lets
us struggle with our weaknesses to reveal His own power.
That understanding comes straight out of Scripture: Paul
wrote, "But we have this treasure in earthen vessels [clay
pots], that the excellency of the power may be of God, and
not of us" (2 Corinthians 4:7, KJV).

It seems to me that *every* believer has at least one
problem with his "clay pot" that is especially troublesome—a nagging irritant or disease—that the Lord
steadfastly refuses to remove. I call them "if onlys."

Look around at your Christian friends. Talk to them about their circumstances. Most will admit to having an "if only" that keeps life from being ideal. If only I didn't have diabetes, or deafness, or sinus problems (or any combination of medical problems). If only my husband and I were not infertile. If only I hadn't gotten into that bad business relationship, or a lawsuit, or a loveless marriage. If only we didn't have a sick child, or a retarded son or daughter, or a troublesome mother-in-law. If only we weren't so strapped financially. If only I hadn't been sexually abused as a child. If only . . . if only God would clear up this one difficulty for me. Yet the problems persist. Regarding those difficulties, the Lord quietly repeats what He said to Paul nearly 2,000 years ago, "My grace is sufficient for you, for my power is made perfect in weakness" (2 Corinthians 12:9).

If I may paraphrase my understanding of that Scripture, He says to us, "Everyone is asked to endure some things that bring discomfort, pain, or sorrow. This is yours. Accept it. Carry it. I will give you the grace to endure it." Thus, life goes on in a state of relative imperfection.

Elisabeth Elliot proposed another explanation for the troubles of mankind in a short essay called "Nevertheless, We Must Run Aground." This is what she wrote:

Have you ever put heart and soul into something, prayed over it, worked at it with a good heart because you believed it to be what God wanted, and finally seen it "run aground?"

The story of Paul's voyage as a prisoner across the Adriatic Sea tells how an angel stood beside him and told him not to be afraid (in spite of winds of hurricane force), for God would spare his life and the lives of all with him on board ship. Paul cheered his guards and fellow-passengers with that word, but added, "Nevertheless, we must run aground on some island" (Acts 27:26).

It would seem that the God who promises to spare all hands might have "done the job right," saved the ship as well, and spared them the ignominy of having to make it to land on the flotsam and jetsam that was left. The fact is He did not, nor does He always spare us.

Heaven is not here, it's There. If we were given all we wanted here, our hearts would settle for this world rather than the next. God is forever luring us up and away from this one, wooing us to Himself and His still invisible Kingdom where we will certainly find what we so keenly long for.

"Running aground," then, is not "the end of the world." But it helps to "Lead us not into temptation"—the temptation complacently to settle for visible things.[1]

There is practical wisdom in these words. All believers will "run aground" at some point in their lives, and they (we) must learn not to panic when the ship grinds

1 "The Elisabeth Elliot Newsletter," September/October 1988.

into a sandbar! That poise under pressure *can* be learned to some degree. Paul wrote in Philippians 4:12, *"I have learned* the secret of being content in any and every situation, whether well fed or hungry, whether living in plenty or in want." It is an acquired serenity.

Unfortunately, there are a few highly visible Christian ministers who confuse people by teaching them there is no need for perseverance and self-control. Why should we practice endurance when health and wealth are available to everyone? By making just the right noises to God, we can tap into His power for trouble-free living. They would transform the King of the Universe into a subservient magician, or a high powered errand boy, who has bound Himself irrevocably to the whims and wishes of us mere mortals. It is a dangerous misrepresentation of Scripture with far-reaching implications for the uninitiated.

I heard a radio minister say on a recent broadcast, "If you have a need, it will be met the moment you ask for help from the Lord. Even as you begin to pray, it is already accomplished. God will solve that problem, whether it is sickness, unemployment, the need for money—whatever. If you have faith, there's no question that God will solve it for you."

It's true that the Lord often does intervene dramatically in the lives of those in difficulty. Scripture could not be more clear about that fact. But *He* will be the determiner of how He responds. No one has the right to make that decision for Him!

After hearing the radio minister make his sweeping

assertion, I went directly to my office at Focus on the Family to attend a staff devotional. I shared what I had heard on the air, to which one of my colleagues said, "It's too bad my dad doesn't know that." His elderly father has suffered a debilitating stroke and now sits partially paralyzed in a wheelchair. This good man, a retired minister who gave his life to Christian service, is going through a tough time. He spends much of his day looking out the window at a golf course on which he will never again walk. It is unconscionable to tell such hurting people that they simply lack the faith to be good as new.

I witnessed another example of this distortion last summer when I visited the United Kingdom. I had gone there to write the early chapters of this book and was deeply enmeshed in the difficult issues we are discussing. Almost on cue, I learned that an American "faith healer" was coming to conduct a highly publicized crusade in London. The media gave this man much wider coverage than he would have received at home, calling him "one of the most popular televangelists in the States." (Actually, he is not very well known here.) Clearly, the British press was convinced that a phony was coming to rip off the gullible in the name of the Lord. That is, indeed, the way it looked.

I will not judge the motives of this televangelist because I am not personally acquainted with him. Perhaps he believes he is doing the Lord's work. But there were aspects of his London crusade that were disturbing. His ad in the tabloids depicted a pair of dark glasses like those worn by the blind. They were cracked. It also featured a white cane, broken in the middle. The caption read, "Some will 'see' miracles for the first time!" Get it? I'm sure thousands of handicapped men, women, and children in London understood the message. It implied an end to suffering was available for those attending the "miracle service."

It's not that God can't heal the blind—or any other disease or deformity. He can and He does. But to my knowledge, He never performs those miracles en masse. Let's put it this way: I have never seen any minister fulfill a promise of universal healing to all comers. Oh, there are some who would have us believe they have a magic touch. But there is reason for skepticism. Furthermore, there's often a disturbing hysteria or a circus atmosphere in the healing services. Such mass-produced miracles affront the sovereignty of God and make a sham of His holy worship.

I'm also convinced that each advocate of universal health and wealth has a little secret down deep in his soul. He has had the experience of praying for a desperately ill family member or a close friend who, nevertheless, did not survive. It has happened to every pastor in every denomination. But this secret is rarely admitted amidst the glitz and exuberance of a "miracle service." Do you agree that there is something not quite honest about concealing those instances when God replies, "It is not my will"?

Returning to the televangelist who came to London, the British media was even more skeptical when the crusade ended. They hired physicians to interview and examine blind and sick people coming out of the "miracle" services. The results were very embarrassing to committed Christians in that great city. It effectively alienated some nonbelievers who might otherwise have been open to the message of the gospel.

There is another reason I am concerned about the teaching of universal health and prosperity. It establishes a level of expectations which will eventually wound and weaken unstable Christians. Someone said, "The man who expects nothing will never be disappointed." By contrast, a person who really believes that all trouble will be swept away for the followers of Christ is left with no logical explanation when God fails to come through. Sooner or later an illness, a business collapse, an accident, or some other misfortune will leave him in dismay.

What is he to believe when he discovers "life as it is" turns out to be very different than "life as it is supposed to be"? He stumbles toward one of several conclusions, all of which are potentially damaging to his faith: (1) God is dead, irrelevant, bored, or uninvolved in the affairs of man; (2) God is angry at me for some sin I've commited; (3) God is whimsical, untrustworthy, unfair or sinister; or (4) God ignored me because I didn't pray enough or display enough faith.

All four of these alternatives serve to isolate that individual from God at precisely the moment when his spiritual need is the greatest. I believe it is a ploy of

Satan to undermine the faith of the vulnerable. And it begins with a theological distortion that promises a stress-free life and a God who always does what He is told. (Note: Some unpleasant experiences in life *do* result from sinful behavior. We'll discuss those circumstances in chapter 9.)

Those who would give glib answers to the awesome question of human suffering have probably not spent much time thinking about it. They certainly have not labored, as I have, in a major children's medical center. There, little kids go through terrifying experiences every day of the week. Some are born in pain and know nothing else. Some have mothers who are cocaine or heroin addicts and come into the world in desperate need of a "fix." For days, the perinatal ward echoes with their pitiful crying. Older children are brought in who have been humiliated, battered and burned by their abusing parents.

Others are like the little brown-eyed girl I remember so vividly in the oncology unit of Children's Hospital of Los Angeles. She was a four-year-old charmer whose parents had thought she was normal and healthy. But the previous day, her mother noticed a protrusion on her side when she was bathing the child. It turned out to be a large malignant tumor. She had only a few months to live. I left her room with a lump in my throat and a longing to go home and hug my healthy boy and girl.

Perhaps you have noticed that life seems blatantly unfair. It pampers some of us and devastates others.

Perhaps this is *the* most disturbing question posed to the thoughtful Christian. How can we explain such an apparent injustice? How can an infinitely loving and just God permit some people to experience lifelong tragedy while others seem to enjoy every good and perfect gift? And what can we conclude when the unfortunate individual is a child? Well, I know the answer offered by theologians—that sickness and death came into the world as a result of sin, and we are all under sentence of death. It comes to some sooner than others. I understand and accept that explanation, even though it leaves us with a troubled spirit.

Admittedly, this explanation of suffering is not very satisfying as we look into the face of a child in pain. It is, however, the best we can do. I've indicated that we can explore the mind of God only so far, and then, inevitably, we run out of brain power. His thoughts are not only unknown to us—they are largely unknowable. He has never made Himself accountable to man, nor will He ever. He will not be crossexamined or interrogated. Nowhere in the Bible does God speak defensively or seek our approval on His actions. He simply says, "Trust me." In His lengthy interchange with Job, not once did Jehovah apologize or attempt to explain the hardship that befell His servant. Still, we are told specifically that God is loving, kind, merciful, long-suffering, gracious, fatherly, patient, etc. So what are we going to do with the discomfort of unanswered questions? It all comes down to the choices posed by Dr. Jim Conway. Either we continue to believe in God's goodness and postpone our questions until we see Him face to face—or we will descend into bitterness and anger for the suffering around us. There are no other alternatives. Inevitably, you see, we circle back to the necessity of faith.

Well, let me end with this: You'll remember the story of Shadrach, Meshach, and Abednego reported in the third chapter of Daniel. They incurred the wrath of Nebuchadnezzar by refusing to fall down and worship the idol he had set up. He made it clear that if they again refused to obey his command, they would be thrown into a "burning fiery furnace." Their response to that murderous threat is one of the most inspiring passages in Scripture:

> *The God we serve is able to save us from it, and he will rescue us from your hand, O king. But even if he does not, we want you to know, O king, that we will not serve your gods or worship the image of gold you have set up.* (Daniel 3:17-18)

What courage these men showed in the very face of death! What conviction! What faith! "God can save us," they said, "but if not, we'll serve Him anyway." That is the biblical prescription in its simplest terms. He can heal the disease that grips my body—but if not, my faith will survive. He can correct my child's handicap, or save my bankrupt business, or bring my son home safely from the war. But if not, I will continue trusting in Him. That's what Job meant when he said, "Though

He slay me, yet will I trust Him" (13:15, NKJV). It is what Paul meant when he said, "Let this mind be in you which was also in Christ Jesus" (Philippians 2:5, NKJV). In verse 8 Paul describes that mind-set: "He humbled himself and became obedient to death—even death on a cross." That utter abandonment to the sovereign will of the Lord is what He wants of His people, even when circumstances seem to swirl out of control. He can rescue—but if not . . . !

To the reader out there who has been diagnosed with a terminal illness, or the parent whose child is in danger, or the recently widowed woman who faces life alone—let me offer a final word of encouragement. Remember when Nebuchadnezzar looked into the blazing furnace and saw four men instead of three, and the fourth looked like the "Son of God"? It is comforting to note that only Shadrach, Meschach, and Abednego came out of the fire. That other Man, whom we believe to have been the Christ, remained there to comfort and protect you and me when we go through our fiery trials.

He will never let you down—but He won't let you off, either!

6

QUESTIONS
AND
ANSWERS

People who are suffering are often filled with questions about life and death, about good and evil, and about the nature of God. Why *do* bad things happen? The following questions express some of the issues and concerns of those going through troubled times.

Q1. **The Lord answered prayer miraculously for my son when he was eight years old. He had open-heart surgery and survived without any permanent problems. But my husband was diagnosed with cancer three years ago, and we prayed for him night and day. Nevertheless, he died last January. I just can't understand why God heard my prayer for our son but allowed my husband to die. Is He there—or isn't He?**

A1. I assure you that He is there, and that your prayers for your husband received no less attention or compassion than those for your endangered son. What you've experienced is evidence of the sovereignty of God. As we have indicated, He will always be the determiner of what is best for those who serve Him.

One of the most dramatic illustrations of this divine nature occurred in the lives of my good friends, Von and Joann Letherer. When Von was just one year old, his parents noticed that he bruised badly whenever he bumped into furniture or even tumbled in his crib. They took him to their doctor, who diagnosed Von with hemophilia—the hereditary "bleeder's disease." His blood lacked the substance necessary to coagulate, actually threatening his life each time he suffered the most minor injury. There was very little treatment for hemophilia in those days, and Von was not expected to live beyond childhood. Indeed, he survived because of prayer, and because of nearly 400 pints of blood transfused by the time he reached the end of adolescence.

During those teen years when Von's life repeatedly hung in the balance, there was a young lady standing by his side. Her name was Joann, and she was his childhood sweetheart. Joann understood very well that Von's future was uncertain, but she loved him dearly. Hemophilia, they decided, was not going to determine the course of their lives. The couple was married when he was 22 and she was 19 years old.

A new crisis occurred several years later when Joann was carrying their second child. She became seriously ill and was diagnosed with Hodgkin's disease, a type of cancer that attacks the lymph glands. It was usually fatal in that day. Although a treatment program had been developed, Joann's pregnancy prevented the doctors from prescribing it for her. She and Von could have aborted their baby, of course, but chose instead to place themselves in the hands of the Lord.

They began asking for a miracle—and promptly received one. Several weeks after the initial diagnosis, the hospital repeated the laboratory and clinical tests. Doctors concluded that there was no sign of Hodgkin's disease in Joann. She has been cancer-free from that day to this.

Now, notice what occurred in this instance. As we have seen, Von was born with a painful, debilitating illness about which his father, a minister, and his mother prayed diligently. They asked repeatedly for God to heal their son. When Von got older, he began praying on his own behalf. Then Joann came along and joined the chorus. Despite these and many other petitions, the Lord chose not to heal Von's hemophilia. At 56 years of age, he is still afflicted with the disorder and suffers daily from immobile joints and related physical difficulties. Von has taken medication every day for many years, just to cope with the pain. Yet his indomitable spirit has been a witness to me and thousands of others through the years.

Why has the Lord been unwilling to heal this good man? I don't know. Some might say that his prayer team lacked faith, except for the fact that Joann was healed in response to their petitions. The same people who asked for intervention in her life were also praying for Von. In one instance the answer was yes, and in the other it was no. And life goes on. The Lord has offered no explanation or interpretation of His response, except by inference, "This is My will for you."

In this and countless other circumstances that occur within the human family, only one conclusion can be drawn: God will do what is best, and we must continue to trust Him regardless of the outcome.

To the woman whose husband recently succumbed to cancer, let me offer this word of encouragement: the Father has not lost track of your circumstances, even though they seem to be swirling out of control. He is there. Hold on to your faith in the midst of these unanswered questions. Someday His purposes will be known and you will have an eternity to talk it over. In the meantime, I pray that the Lord will help you cope with this tragic loss of, or should I say temporary separation from, your partner and friend.

Q2. **I know God is able to do miracles and even raise the dead. I have to admit, however, that it is hard to depend on Him when I'm going through dark times. Does this reveal a lack of faith?**

A2. Most of us struggle to "be anxious for nothing" when we are agitated or frightened by events in our lives. Still, we can learn to let God be God and accept His direction and judgment. But in direct response to your question, I think you may be confusing the concepts of faith and trust. There is a very old illustration that brings these two ideas into sharp focus. It goes like this: Imagine yourself near the beautiful and dangerous Niagara Falls on the border between Canada and upstate New York. Suppose a circus performer has strung a rope across the falls with the intention of pushing a wheelbarrow to the other side. If he loses his balance, he will surely drown or be crushed in the churning waters below. Just before stepping on the rope, the stunt man turns to you and says, "Do you think I can accomplish this feat?"

You reply that his reputation has preceded him and that you fully believe he has the ability to walk the tightrope. In other words, you have *faith* that he will succeed.

But then he says, "If you really believe I can do it, how about getting in the wheelbarrow and crossing to the other side with me?" To accept that invitation would be an example of remarkable *trust*.

It is not difficult for some of us to believe that God is capable of performing mighty deeds. After all, He created the entire universe from nothingness. He has the power to do anything He chooses. Having faith in Him can be a fairly straightforward thing.

To demonstrate trust, however, takes the relationship a step farther. It involves the element of risk. It requires us to depend on Him to keep his promises, even when proof is not provided. It is continuing to believe when the evidence points in the opposite direction. Yes, it is getting into the wheelbarrow and making the perilous journey across the falls. I'm convinced that faith in moments of crisis is insufficient, unless we are also willing to trust our very lives to His care. That is a learned response, and some people find it more difficult than others by reason of temperament.

Q3. **There are times when I feel so close to the Lord and I can sense His approval on my life. On**

other occasions, it seems like He is a million miles away. How can I have any stability in my spiritual life when the Lord's assurance and presence are so inconstant?

A3. His presence is *not* inconstant. It is your perception of Him that comes and goes. If your spiritual walk is dependent on the ebb and flow of emotion, your confidence as a believer will pitch and roll like a ship on a stormy sea. Very little in human experience is as undependable as the way we feel from day to day. That's why our faith must be grounded in a solid commitment of the will, in our prayer life, and in a careful study of Scripture.

Another factor is extremely important in understanding God's intervention in human affairs. It deals with the natural rhythm to our lives—the regular progression of emotions and circumstances from positive to negative to positive. We are rarely granted more than about two weeks of tranquility before something goes wrong. Either the roof springs a leak, or the Ford throws a rod, or the kids get the chicken pox, or business reverses occur. Mark Twain said life is just one darn thing after another. That's just the way it goes in this imperfect world.

If it's any consolation to those of you who have also been dragged up and down the emotional roller coaster, it is apparent from Scripture that even Jesus experienced this fluctuation. His ministry began officially at the Jordan River, where He was baptized by

John. That must have been the most exhilarating day of his 30 years on earth. Matthew 3:16-17 tells us, "As soon as Jesus was baptized, he went up out of the water. At that moment heaven was opened, and he saw the Spirit of God descending like a dove and lighting on him. And a voice from heaven said, 'This is my Son, whom I love; with him I am well pleased.'"

What an incredible experience that must have been for the young Messiah. There are no words to describe what it meant to be ordained and blessed by the Father in this manner. But note that the next verse says, "Then Jesus was led by the Spirit into the desert to be tempted by the devil" (Matthew 4:1). Isn't it interesting that Jesus was taken from the most emotionally exhilarating experience of his life directly into one of the most terrible ordeals he would ever encounter—a 40-day battle with Satan? Observe, also, that He didn't wander into the desert. He didn't even go there by His own design. He was *led* there by the Spirit to be tempted by the devil!

The upheaval in Jesus' life was only beginning. In a sense, His entire ministry is characterized by that fluctuation. After His difficult period in the wilderness, He began to receive the adulation of the crowds as word spread that a "prophet" was in their midst. Can't you imagine the scenes of hysteria as sick and deformed people pressed to get near Him?

Then the chief priests and the Pharisees began plotting to kill Jesus. He became a hated man and, eventually, a wanted criminal. They tried to embarrass and intimidate Him wherever He went. Back and forth came the praise of the common people and the animosity of the religious leaders.

Let's move to the events surrounding Jesus' final days on earth. Multitudes came to greet Him as He approached Jerusalem, shouting, "Hosanna: Blessed is the King of Israel that cometh in the name of the Lord" (John 12:13, KJV). A few days later, however, He went through the terrible ordeal surrounding His persecution and trial. The same people who had worshiped Him now clamored for His execution. Then He was crucified between two thieves on Mount Calvary. This darkest day in human history was followed three days later by the most wonderful news ever given to mankind. Soon, 120 disciples received the baptism of the Holy Spirit at Pentecost, and the church was born. That was followed by incredible persecution of the saints and the martyrdom of many. There was good news one day and bad news the next. James was killed, but Peter was rescued. The early Christians went through high moments and low times as they labored to establish the church.

What I've tried to illustrate through the vicissitudes of Jesus' ministry is that there is no stability or predictability in this imperfect world. It is that way for you and me, too. We must expect the unexpected—the unsettling—the irritating. One day we'll ride high above the fray and the next we could slide under the door. So whence cometh the stability in such a topsy-turvy world? It is found only by anchoring our faith on the unchanging, everlasting Lord, whose promises never fail and whose love is all encompassing. Our joy and our hope can be as steady as the sunrise even when the happenings around us are transitioning from wonderful to tragic. That's what Scripture teaches us, and His peace is there for those who choose to take it.

Q4. **I've often heard that God will not abandon us when we go through the fiery trial. But I don't know what that really means. You've shown that He still lets us go through some hard times. What can we expect from Him in the stressful moments?**

A4. I may lack the words to describe what occurs to the faithful in times of personal crisis. It is virtually inexpressible. Let it be said, simply, that there is often a quiet awareness in the midst of chaos that the Lord is there and He is still in control. Millions of people have reported this persistent presence when life was systematically unraveling. On other occasions, He permits us to see evidence of His love at the critical moment of need.

I recall today that tragic time in 1987 when my four friends were killed in a private plane crash. We had been together the night before, and I had prayed for their safety on the journey home (see photo following page 134). They took off early the next morning on their way to Dallas, but never made it. I can never forget that telephone call indicating the wreckage had been found in a remote canyon—but there were no survivors! I loved those men like brothers, and I was staggered by the loss.

I was asked by the four families to speak briefly at their funeral. The untimely deaths of such vibrant and deeply loved men seemed to scream for an explanation. Where was God in their passing? Why did He let this happen? Why would He take such godly men from their families and leave them reeling in grief and pain? There were no answers to these agonizing questions, and I did not try to produce them. But I did say that God had not lost control of their lives, and that He wanted us to trust Him when nothing made sense. His presence was very near.

As we exited the sanctuary that day, I stood talking with loved ones and friends who had gathered to say good-bye. Suddenly, someone pointed to the sky and exclaimed, "Look at that!" Suspended directly above the steeple was a small rainbow in the shape of a smile. There had been no precipitation that day and no more than a few fleecy clouds. Yet this beautiful little rainbow appeared above the church. We learned later that it had been hovering there through most of the funeral service. It was as though the Lord was saying to the grieving wives and children, "Be at peace. Your men are with Me, and all is well. I know you don't understand, but I want you to trust Me. I'm going to take care of you, and this rainbow is a sign to remember."

A gentleman residing near the church, Mr. William Mueller, had the presence of mind to photograph it at that moment. When it was developed, we saw what no one recognized at the time (see photo preceding page 135). As you can see, there is a small private plane cradled near the center of the rainbow.

Cynics and nonbelievers will say the rainbow and the plane are coincidences that have no spiritual significance. They are entitled to their opinion. But for every member of four wounded families, and certainly for me, the Lord used that phenomenon to convey His peace to us all. He has fulfilled His promise to take care of those four courageous widows and their children.

There are other examples which beg to be shared. Sandra Lund and her family survived Hurricane Andrew in south Florida by spending the night in a shelter. Then they returned to their home the next morning to find everything destroyed except some of the interior walls. As a bewildered Sandra strolled through the rubble, she found a note she had taped in what had been the kitchen. It was still in place, and read, "For I have learned in whatsoever state I am, therewith to be content." On the remaining bathroom wall was another verse she had penned, "O give thanks to the Lord for He is good." Sandra got the message.

Finally, I experienced that same presence in the midst of another kind of storm. On August 15, 1990, I was playing an early morning round of basketball, as was my custom. At 54 years of age, I thought I was in great physical condition. I had recently undergone a medical examination and was pronounced to be in excellent health. I could play basketball all day with men 25 years my junior. But there were unpleasant surprises in store for me on that particular morning. I was just a few feet from where NBA legend Pete Maravich had died in my arms two years earlier. (That gym floor is hallowed for me now, as you can understand.)

Suddenly, I was stricken by a moderate pain in the center of my chest. I excused myself, telling my friends I didn't feel well. Then I foolishly drove alone to a nearby emergency clinic and booked a room. This was the same hospital, by the way, where my father was taken after his heart attack 21 years earlier. So began 10 days that would change my life.

It is a great shock for a man who still thinks of himself as "Joe College" to acknowledge that he is looking death in the face. It took a while for that thought to sink in. My first afternoon in the cardiac care unit was spent working on a new book I was writing with Gary Bauer entitled *Children at Risk*. I had the nurses tape five possible cover designs on the wall and votes were taken as hospital staff came through. I wrote throughout the afternoon. But when the enzyme report came back about midnight and confirmed that I had suffered some damage to the heart muscle, I knew I was in serious trouble. It was later confirmed that my left anterior descending artery, the one cardiologists call the "widow maker," was entirely blocked.

Hospital staff came at me from every direction. Tubes and IVs were strung all over me. An automatic blood pressure machine pumped frantically on my arm every five minutes throughout the night, and a nurse delicately suggested that I not move unless absolutely necessary. That does tend to get your attention. As I lay there in the darkness listening to the *beep-beep-beep* of the oscilloscope, I began to think very clearly about the people I loved and what things did and did not really matter.

Fortunately, the damage sustained to my heart proved to be minor, and I have fully recovered. I exercise an hour each morning, seven days a week, and I'm eating some of the finest birdseed money can buy. I used to be a junk food junky, and I'm still not thrilled about cauliflower, alfalfa, squash and other things that would have made me gag a few years ago. Nor am I yet convinced that God intended for full-grown men to eat like rabbits and gophers. Surely there is a place in his scheme of things for enchiladas, pizza, donuts, ice cream, and cherry pie. Nevertheless, I'm playing by the rules these days. My diet is designed by some very petite nutritionists who look like they've never eaten a real meal in their lives. It's a sad story, I tell you, but I sure feel wonderful. Pass the yogurt, please.

During those last nine days in the cardiac care unit, I was keenly aware of the implications of my illness. I had watched my father and four of his brothers die of the same disease. I understood full well that my time on this earth could be drawing to an end. Still, I felt the kind of inexplicable peace I described earlier. There were thousands of people praying for me around the country, and I seemed to be cradled in the presence of the Lord. I had lived my life in such a way as to be ready for that moment, and I knew that my sins had been forgiven. That is a priceless awareness when everything is on the line.

There was one brief period, however, when my confidence began to crumble. The day before I was discharged, I underwent an angiogram to determine the nature of my arterial network and the extent of my heart damage. The initial report from that procedure was much more threatening than would later be confirmed, and those ominous findings did not escape my notice. I saw the concern on the faces of technicians. I heard a young Japanese medical resident read the report and mutter in broken English, "Oh, dat not good." She might as well have said, "Dis is gonna kill you."

I was taken back to my room and left to ponder what was going on. For the first time in the long ordeal, anxiety swept over me. Modern medicine can terrorize those it seeks to serve, as laboratory reports and tentative diagnoses trickle in. You can adjust to anything if given time. It's the uncertainty that rattles the nerves. I was going through that drill while waiting for my cardiologist to come by. That's when I uttered a brief and ineloquent prayer from the depths of my soul. I said, "Lord, you know where I am right now. And you know that I am upset and very lonely. Would you send someone who can help me?"

A short time later, my good friend Dr. Jack Hayford, pastor of The Church on the Way in Los Angeles, unexpectedly walked through the door. Many of you know him from his writings and television ministry. We greeted each other warmly, and then I said, "Jack, your church is on the other side of town. Why did you take the time to come see me today?" I didn't tell him about my prayer.

I'll never forget his reply. He said, "Because the Lord told me you were lonely."

That's the kind of God we serve. He lovingly sent that good man to see me even before I had asked for help. Now admittedly, the Lord doesn't always solve our problems instantaneously, and He sometimes permits us to walk through the valley of the shadow of death. Eventually we'll all take that journey. But He is there with us even in the darkest hours, and we can never escape His encompassing love. I was warmly embraced by it throughout my hospitalization, even in the darkest hour.

Psalm 73:23-26 meant so much to me during my convalescence. I think you will understand why. It reads:

> Yet I am always with you; you hold me by my right hand. You guide me with your counsel, and afterward you will take me into glory. Whom have I in heaven but you? And earth has nothing I desire besides you. My flesh and my heart may fail, but God is the strength of my heart and my portion forever.

Q5. Do you believe the Lord still performs miracles today, or has the era of supernatural intervention passed?

A5. I have no doubt that miracles still occur every day, although, as indicated earlier, I'm suspicious of people who attempt to market them on demand. I have been privileged to witness some incredible evidences of God's power in my life and in the experience of those with whom I am close. One of the most miraculous events happened to my friend, Jim Davis, when he and his family visited Yellowstone National Park in 1970. Jim was a guest on the Focus on the Family broadcast some time later, and he shared that experience with our listeners. These are his approximate words on that occasion:

> *My wife and I were both raised in Christian families, and we were taught the power of prayer. But we were not living very godly lives. We did not pray together or have a family altar in our home. About that time, she made a wonderful commitment to the Lord and began praying for me. She bought me a research Bible, and I began to get into the Word. Things started to change in my heart, but I still wasn't mature spiritually.*
>
> *That summer, we went on a vacation to Yellowstone Park with four other couples. Several of these friends went fishing the next day in an aluminum boat, and one of the ladies hooked a trout. She leaned over to net the fish, and her glasses fell off. They immediately sank to the bottom of the lake. She was very disturbed by the loss because it was the beginning of their vacation, and she could not*

drive or read without the glasses. She also got severe headaches when she didn't wear them.

That night, everyone was talking about the glasses and how unfortunate it was that they were lost. Then my wife said, "No sweat. Jim is a great scuba diver. He'll go out and find them for you."

"Hey, thanks a lot," I said. "Do you know that Yellowstone Lake has 172 miles of shoreline, and every tree is coniferous and looks exactly the same? There's no way I can get a fix on where you guys were when the glasses went overboard. Besides, the water is very, very cold—50 degrees. They won't even allow you to water-ski out there. And I don't have a wet suit—just a pair of fins and a snorkel."

My objections fell on deaf ears. She told me privately that she intended to pray that the Lord would help me find those glasses.

Yeah, sure, I thought.

The next morning we got in the boat and headed about a half mile out from shore.

"Uh, where do you think you dropped them?" I asked.

"It seems like about here," someone said.

Well, I got in the water, and it was freezing. I took hold of a rope, and the boat dragged me along the surface as I looked at the bottom. The water was about 10 feet deep and crystal clear. We made a swath about 50 feet long and then turned and worked our way back. After about 20 minutes of this search, I was just chilled to the bone. I prayed a little prayer and said, Lord, if You know where those glasses are, I sure wish You'd tell me. I wasn't convinced He knew. It's a very big lake.

But a little voice in my mind said, I know exactly where they are. Get in the boat, and I'll take you to them. Well, I didn't tell anyone about this message because I was too embarrassed to say it. But about 20 minutes later I was just shivering, and I said, Lord, if You still know where those glasses are, I'll get in the boat.

I called out to my friends and said, "We're in the wrong place. They're over there."

I got in the boat and pointed to a spot that I thought the Lord was telling me about. The driver said, "No, we weren't out that far." But we kept going, and I said, "Stop. Right here. This is the place."

I jumped back in the water and looked down. We were right on top of those glasses. I dove to the bottom and came up with the prize. It was one of the clearest answers to prayer I've ever experienced, and it set me on fire spiritually. It was also an incredible witness to my wife and all my friends. And I'll never forget those sparkling glasses at the bottom of Yellowstone Lake.

As dramatic as this story is, I can personally vouch for its authenticity as Jim told it. There are many witnesses who remember that remarkable day on Yel-

James Dobson, at right, with four friends soon to be lost in a plane crash. They are, from left to right, Dr. Trevor Mabrey, Hugo Schoellkopf, Creath Davis, and George Clark.

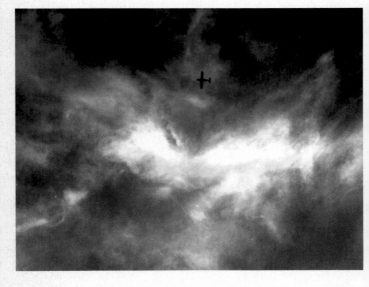

Rainbow as it appeared during the funeral. Note the small private airplane, which was not noticed until the photograph was developed.

lowstone Lake. What I don't know is why the Lord chose to reveal Himself in that way, or why He doesn't do it more often. Clearly, He has plans and purposes to which we are not privy.

I can't resist sharing another incident that ranks as one of the most interesting examples of God's intervention I've ever heard. It occurred in 1945, shortly after the end of the Second World War. A young associate pastor named Cliff and his fiancée, Billie, were anxious to get married, even though they had very little money. They managed to scrape together enough funds for a simple wedding and two train tickets to a city where he had been asked to hold a revival with a friend. By combining this responsibility with their honeymoon, they thought they could make it. They planned to stay at a nearby resort hotel.

The couple got off the train and took a bus to the hotel, only to learn that it had been taken over by the military for use as a rehabilitation center. It was no longer open for guests. There they were, stranded in an unfamiliar city with only a few dollars between them. There was little to do but attempt to hitch a ride on the nearby highway. Soon a car pulled over, and the driver asked them where they wanted to go.

"We don't know," they said, and explained their predicament. The man was sympathetic and said perhaps he could offer a suggestion. A few miles down the road was a grocery store that was owned by a woman he knew. She had a couple of empty rooms upstairs and might be willing to let them stay there inexpensively. They were in no position to be choosy.

The lady rented them a room for five dollars, and they moved in. During their first day in residence, the new bride spent the afternoon practicing the piano, and Cliff played the trombone he had brought with him. The proprietor of the store sat rocking in a chair, listening to the music. When she realized they were Christians, she referred them to a friend, who invited them to spend the rest of their honeymoon in his home. Several days later, the host mentioned that a young evangelist was speaking at a youth rally at a nearby Christian conference center. They were invited to attend.

That night, it so happened that the regular song leader was sick, and Cliff was asked to take charge of the music for the service. What an historic occasion it was! The evangelist turned out to be a very young Rev. Billy Graham. The groom was Cliff Barrows. They met that evening for the first time, and a lifetime partnership was formed. As the Christian world knows so well, Cliff and his wife, Billie, have been members of the Billy Graham Evangelistic Association ever since that evening and have been used by the Lord in thousands of crusades all around the world. I suppose Paul Harvey would say, "And now you know . . . the *rest* of the story."

Isn't it amazing the lengths to which the Lord went to bring these now inseparable team members together? Some would call their meeting a coincidence, but I disagree. I recognize the hand of God when I see it.

Do miracles still occur today as they did in Bible times? Yes, but they usually take place in such a manner as to preserve the need for faith. Even those who witness them must choose whether or not to believe in their validity. I choose to believe!

Q6. **Whenever Christians talk about pain and suffering, someone can be counted on to quote Romans 8:28, "And we know that in all things God works for the good of those who love him, who have been called according to his purpose." But how can that be true literally? You have acknowledged that Christians go through the same kind of suffering that unbelieving people do. So how can it be said that all their difficulties somehow "work together for good"?**

A6. First, it must be noted from this Scripture that Paul didn't say all things were good. He wasn't claiming that death, sickness, and sorrow were really positives in disguise. But he did tell us that God has promised to take these hardships and bring good from them. As long as what happens to me is within the perfect will of the Father, I have no reason to fear—even if it costs me my life. It is an article of our faith that we can trust Him to do what is best, even if it appears contrary to our own wishes or the prevailing attitudes of the day.

I'll answer the question a different way. The laws of physics tell us that energy in the universe is never lost. It is simply transformed from one state to another. So it is with human experience. Nothing is ever lost entirely. God uses every happening to accomplish His divine purposes. For example, I mentioned in chapter 1 that Jim Elliot and his companions were speared to death by Waorani Indians in Ecuador. Their sacrifice seemed like an unmitigated tragedy and a total waste of human life. In God's scheme of things, however, it had a purpose. Each of those Indians came to know Jesus Christ as his personal Savior in the years that followed. The gospel was firmly planted among their tribesmen. Thus, Elliot and his fellow missionaries will rejoice throughout eternity with the men who took their lives. That is "good." Romans 8:28, then, must be interpreted from this eternal perspective, rather than a temporal, earthbound point of view.

There are innumerable other examples. Remember the death of Stephen, the first believer to be martyred in the days following the crucifixion of Jesus? What was accomplished for God by the terrible stoning of this faithful apostle? Well, it caused early believers to flee from Roman persecution. As they went, they carried the news of Jesus' death and resurrection to the far reaches of the known world. The "church" was planted in countless communities and cities where the Good News would not otherwise have been heard.

Let's cite an illustration closer to home. A few months ago, we received a phone call here at Focus on the Family from a Mr. Greg Krebs. He wanted to get a message through to me, and this is what he told our telephone representative. Mr. Krebs and his wife have a 21-year-old son named Chris, whom they had been advised to abort when still in the womb. They chose to give him life, and he was born with cerebral palsy. He is also profoundly retarded. His parents do not regret their decision to bring him into the world, because they believe that all life is precious. They are thankful for this son, who has touched their lives in warm and wonderful ways.

"God has used him as he is," Mr. Krebs said.

Then he described something that happened when Chris was just seven years old. He said, "My wife worked in a hospital at the time, and I had taken Chris with me to pick her up. She was late getting off, so Chris and I waited for her in one of the family rooms. There was another man there who was not well dressed and, in fact, was a little smelly. I went to the nurses' station to ask how much longer my wife would be, and when I returned, I saw Chris sitting by the man. The man was sobbing, and I wondered what Chris had done to offend him. I began to apologize.

"'I'm sorry if my son offended you,' I said.

"The man replied, 'Offended me? Offended me? Your son is the only person who has hugged me in the last 20 years!'

"I realized at that moment Chris had a more Christlike love for this man than I did."

Thank you, Mr. and Mrs. Krebs, for loving and valuing your son despite his limitations. I agree wholeheartedly that there is no "junk" in God's value system. He loves every one of us the same, and He uses each person—even the profoundly retarded—to accomplish some part of His purpose. He will also use your pain, although it is not always immediately possible to interpret it.

To repeat my thesis, when we submit ourselves to the sovereign will of the Lord, we can say with confidence that in all things—yes, in *all* things—God works for the good of them who love Him, who have been called according to His purpose.

7

THE
ADVERSITY
PRINCIPLE

Let me turn a corner, now, and approach this important topic of "faith under fire" from another direction.

From the time I was 10 years of age and read my first book about the stars and planets, I have had a fascination with the subject of astronomy. What captured my imagination was the relative size of those twinkling little lights above us. The earth, I discovered, was a mere peanut compared to the larger bodies in our neighborhood. I am still awestruck by the unbelievable dimensions of God's creation. How does one grasp the meaning of a visible universe that is at least 30 billion light years across and composed of perhaps 100 billion galaxies, each containing hundreds of billions of stars? It is breathtaking to consider what exists there in the silent sky. One of the objects relatively near to us, a star named Epsilon, is actually larger than the orbit of the planet Pluto in our solar system! If it were hollow, it could contain more than 2.3 billion of our suns!

King David, who could have known nothing about modern astronomy, was keenly aware of the Lord's marvelous work in creation. He wrote, "The heavens declare the glory of God; the skies proclaim the work of his hands. Day after day they pour forth speech; night after night they display knowledge" (Psalm 19:1-2). Indeed they do! I suppose that is why the study of astronomy still holds such excitement for me. It *de-*

clares God's magnificent glory like no other field of inquiry. After exploring what the Creator has done and how He continues to control the vast reaches of the cosmos, I find it easy to trust Him with the concerns of my life. Somehow, it seems like He just might be able to handle them.

I remember with fondness a story about Albert Einstein and his speculation about time and space. One day he was interacting with some of his brighter students about God and whether or not He exists. Einstein then asked them this provocative question: "What percent of the total knowledge of the universe do you suppose we now possess?" They gave him various estimates, averaging about 2 percent. The old physicist replied, "I think your guesses are high, but I'll accept that figure of 2 percent. Now tell me, what are the chances that God exists in the other 98?" A very good question, to be sure!

In my further reading about astronomy some years ago, I came across the work of a man named Dr. Stephen Hawking. He is an astrophysicist at Cambridge University and perhaps the most intelligent man on earth. The mantle of Einstein has fallen on his shoulders, and he has worn it with dignity. He has advanced the general theory of relativity farther than any person since the old man died. Dr. Hawking is also credited with mathematical calculations suggesting the existence of black holes in space and other widely acclaimed theories.

Unfortunately, Dr. Hawking is afflicted with a rare

degenerative neuromuscular disorder called amyotrophic lateral sclerosis (ALS syndrome), or Lou Gehrig's disease. It will eventually take his life. He has been confined to a wheelchair for years, where he can do little more than sit and think. He cannot even write down the mathematical formulae that govern the progression of his thoughts. *Omni* magazine said of Hawking back in 1979, "His mind is a blackboard. He memorizes the long strings of equations that give life to his ideas, then dictates the results to his colleagues or secretary—a feat that has been compared to Beethoven's writing an entire symphony in his head or Milton's dictating *Paradise Lost* to his daughter."

In more recent years, Hawking has lost the ability even to speak, and now he communicates by means of a computer that is operated from the tiniest movement of his fingertips. Quoting *Omni* again: "He is too weak to write, feed himself, comb his hair, fix his glasses—all this must be done for him. Yet this most dependent of all men has escaped invalid status. His personality shines through the messy details of his existence."[1]

That acceptance of catastrophic illness is what makes Stephen Hawking of interest in the present discussion, even though he does not believe in the God of the Bible. He might be a deist, although he wrote a book in 1988 entitled *A Brief History of Time* in which he labored to explain away the need for a Creator. Nevertheless, what Hawking learned from his disability is

1 *Omni* (February 1979): 46.

remarkable and can be enlightening to those of us who live by faith.

He said that before he became ill, he had very little interest in life. He called it a "pointless existence" resulting from sheer boredom. He drank too much and did very little work. Then he learned he had ALS syndrome and was not expected to live more than two years. The ultimate effect of that diagnosis, beyond its initial shock, was extremely positive. He claimed to have been happier after he was afflicted than before. How can that be understood? Hawking provided the answer.

He said, "When one's expectations are reduced to zero, one really appreciates everything that one does have." This is the point I made in the first chapter of this book. Stated another way, contentment in life is determined, in part, by what a person anticipates from it. To a man like Hawking who thought he would soon die quickly, everything takes on meaning—a sunrise or a walk in a park or the laughter of children. Suddenly, each small pleasure becomes precious. By contrast, those who believe life owes them a free ride are often discontent with its finest gifts.

Hawking also said this about his physical limitations: "If you're disabled, you should pour your energies into those areas where you are not handicapped. You should concentrate on what you can do well, and not mourn over what you cannot do. And it is very important not to give in to self-pity. If you're disabled and you feel sorry for yourself, then no one is going to have much to do with you. A physically handicapped person certainly cannot afford to be psychologically handicapped as well."[2]

Another way of expressing Hawking's point is that a person faced with extreme hardship must press himself to get tougher. Whining and self-pity, as logical as they seem, are deadly indulgences. An individual in crisis will either grow stronger or become demoralized. Within certain limits, of course, adversity can have a positive effect on people by helping to build character. For Christians, Scripture says it develops and enhances that precious characteristic called faith (James 1:2-4).

Biologists have long recognized this concept, which we'll call the adversity principle, at work in the world of plants and animals. As strange as it seems, habitual well-being is not advantageous to a species. An existence without challenge takes its toll on virtually every living thing. Just look at the flabby animals in a zoo, for example. Food is delivered to them every day, and they need do nothing but lie around and yawn. Or consider a tree planted in a rain forest. Because water is readily available, it does not have to extend its root system more than a few feet below the surface. Consequently, it is often poorly anchored and can be toppled by a minor windstorm. But a mesquite tree planted in a hostile and arid land must send its roots down 30 feet or more in search of water. Not even a gale can blow it over. Its unfriendly habitat actually contributes to stability and vigor.

It is also relevant to the human family. Some of the

2 *Caltech News* (December 1975).

most noble examples of courage have occurred in countries undergoing severe pressure. The shattered nations of Europe in the 1940s come to mind in this context. All wars are horrible, and I'm certainly not minimizing the suffering they cause. World War II claimed 50 million lives and virtually destroyed a continent before it was over. Still, those who survived the ordeal were forced to adapt in order to endure their season in hell. Look at the effect of that adaptation.

The Germans were subjected to terrible devastation near the end of the war, just as they had inflicted it on others. Some of their larger cities were bombed around the clock—by the Americans throughout the day and by the British at night. Death and destruction were everywhere. Food was extremely scarce, as were all the essentials to life. By the end of the war, 80 percent of the men born in 1922 were dead, spreading grief and heartache throughout the land. These tragedies resulted from Nazi aggression, of course, but the suffering by individual German families was no less real. What is remarkable from today's perspective is the degree to which they hung tough. They did not crack! Even in the winter of 1945, when factories had been bombed, trains were destroyed and bridges shattered, the productivity of the nation was still nearly 80 percent of prewar capacity. Morale remained high. They continued to exhibit a national resolve—a collective commitment to the war effort—even when Allied armies were tightening the noose around Berlin.

No less impressive was Britain's record during the

war. Churchill rallied the people to personal heroism. He began by addressing their expectations, offering them nothing "but blood, toil, sweat and tears." That helped steel them against hardship. In the darkest days of the blitz when their beloved homeland was in imminent danger of invasion, the Brits dug in. No one was certain whether or not Hitler and his minions could be stopped. Yet England's most popular song in that ominous hour expressed hope—not fear. It was called "The White Cliffs of Dover," referring to a coastal area that bristled with guns, planes, and radar equipment. These are the lyrics that I remember from childhood:

There'll be Bluebirds over
The white cliffs of Dover
Tomorrow, just you wait and see
There'll be love and laughter
And peace ever after,
Tomorrow, when the world is free
The shepherd will tend his sheep
The valley will bloom again
And Jimmy will go to sleep
In his own little room again
There'll be Bluebirds over
The white cliffs of Dover
Tomorrow, just you wait and see.

This song came to symbolize the courage of a people looking past death and sacrifice to a better day ahead. Churchill called that era "their finest hour."

This same indomitable spirit was evident in many of the other war-torn countries during that time. It reached a culmination in the city of Leningrad (now called St. Petersburg), where the Russian people endured horrible deprivation during an 872-day siege by German and Finnish armies. More than 650,000 Leningraders died in 1942 alone, mostly from starvation, disease, and shelling by distant guns. But the survivors refused to surrender to tyranny. Their response to unimaginable horror stands as one of the world's most striking examples of raw human courage. St. Petersburg is called the "Hero City" today.

If it is accurate to say that hard times often lead to emotional and physical toughness, then the opposite must also be valid. And, indeed, it is. Easy living and abundance often produce a certain underlying weakness. With due respect to my fellow countrymen here in the United States, I believe we have been made soft and vulnerable by materialism and ease. Prolonged prosperity, at least as compared with the rest of the world, has given us a seductive love of comfort. I wonder at times if we could tolerate the level of deprivation that is common for most of the human family. We seem to be having enough trouble just coping with the routine pressures of living.

Russian philosopher and author Aleksandr Solzhenitsyn recognized this national weakness shortly after he was exiled to the United States from what was then the Soviet Union. In a now-famous address delivered at Harvard University on June 8, 1978, he referred to the softness that permeated the democracies. He said it was apparent to him that Western nations were not as secure and stable as they appeared. Telltale signs of social disintegration were evident in the culture. He referred specifically to the absence of great statesmen and to lawless behavior, such as the rioting and looting that occurred when a power outage momentarily darkened our cities. Solzhenitsyn gave numerous examples before concluding, "The smooth surface film must be very thin, [because] the social system [is] quite unstable and unhealthy."

The short fuse observed by Solzhenitsyn is even more characteristic of Americans today. It takes so little to set our nerves on edge. Drivers on Los Angeles freeways sometimes shoot each other for the most insignificant insult. Violence of all kinds permeates society. The 1992 riots in Los Angeles and other cities shocked the world with their wanton brutality and vandalism. Alcoholism, immorality, drug abuse, family disintegration, child molestation, pornography, delinquency, homosexuality, and gambling are more pervasive than ever. The culture appears to be cooking along just below the simmer point. Very little is required to boil it over. And this is occurring in relatively *good* times. It would appear, indeed, that prosperity is a greater test of character than is adversity.

Does this principle operate within a Christian context as well? There's no doubt about it. Look at the church in Eastern Europe compared with that in Western Europe. Before the collapse of communism and the opening of the borders, the Christian community was much stronger under totalitarian domination than in the warmth of freedom. That fact amazes me. The church was alive and well in Poland, Czechoslovakia, Romania, and East Germany, where there were no seminaries, no Christian conferences, very few Bibles or supportive literature, and no religious radio, television, or films. Communist oppression of believers was intense. Pastors and priests shepherded six or eight parishes because of the shortage of trained leaders. Being a Christian carried a big price tag. Yet faith not only prevailed in this harsh environment. It flourished.

By contrast, religious commitment languished in the freedom of Western Europe. Apathy was especially evident in countries where the church was supported by public funds, such as Denmark, Sweden, Norway, and Greece. One might conclude from this recent history that the best way to kill or weaken the church is to remove all challenge to its existence.

Let's bring the adversity principle closer to home. How does it apply to you and me? Could it be that our heavenly Father permits His children to struggle in order to keep us strong? I firmly believe that to be true. That is precisely what James told the Jewish-Christians in the first century: "Consider it pure joy, my brothers, whenever you face trials of many kinds, because you know that the testing of your faith develops perseverance" (James 1:2-3). Paul echoed that theme in his letter to the Romans: "We also rejoice in our sufferings, because we know that suffering produces perseverance; perseverance, character; and character, hope" (Romans 5:3-4).

Jesus said it even more plainly, "If anyone would come after me, he must deny himself and take up his cross and follow me" (Matthew 16:24). He also said, "For whoever wants to save his life will lose it, but whoever loses his life for me will find it" (v. 25). Those words leave little room for doubt. Jesus wants us to be committed and disciplined and tough. He also warned about the dangers of the soft life. This, I believe, is what he meant when He said, "It is easier for a camel to go through the eye of a needle than for a rich man to enter the kingdom of God" (Mark 10:25). He did not mean that God sets up a different—and more difficult—standard by which wealthy people are judged. Rather, He was acknowledging that affluence can make us dependent on ease and comfort. As such, it is highly seductive. A person who grows accustomed to life's good things may not be drawn naturally to the sacrificial way of the Cross. Like the rich young ruler who walked away from Jesus, a wealthy person may find it more difficult to follow this Master who calls us to make the supreme sacrifice.

Not only is affluence dangerous, but so is the adulation of our fellow men. If you want to know what a person is made of, grant him a high degree of social status and admiration. His hidden character will soon be apparent for all to see. Solomon wrote, "The crucible for silver and the furnace for gold, but man is tested by the praise he receives" (Proverbs 27:21).

From these Scriptures and many others, it should be obvious that the Christian life was never intended to be a stroll through a rose garden. That idyllic existence ended when Adam and Eve were evicted from the Garden of Eden. Since then, life has been a challenge for us all. I'll bet you already knew that.

I was going through a period of challenge several years ago when frustrations were coming by the boat-loads. I felt like Job when the bearers of bad news were standing in line to tell their stories. It had been that kind of month. Then one night when Shirley had gone out of town to attend a conference, I decided to visit my favorite restaurant—a local drive-through hamburger stand. (This was before my cardiologist and my wife got together and destroyed one of the finer joys of living.)

I jumped into our son's Honda, not remembering that I had canceled the insurance on his car when he went back to college. I had gone about three blocks when it dawned on me that I was driving without liability coverage. *One stupid mistake and we could lose our house,* I thought. I was only two blocks from the drive-in, so I slowed the car to a crawl. At each corner I virtually stopped, looking both ways before inching on down the road. I'm sure people thought I was either senile or weird—or both.

I arrived safe and sound at the beloved IN 'N' OUT Hamburger and heaved a sigh of relief. "May I have your order, please?" said a muffled adolescent voice from the little black box. I told the guy what I wanted and then drove forward to the take-out window. Soon, a sack of great-smelling stuff was handed to me and I reached for it. There I was, hanging out the window nice and loose—when an elderly lady lost control of the Mercedes behind me. Her foot slipped off the brake and crammed the accelerator. It was like a Sherman tank hitting a baby buggy! Suddenly, Ryan's Honda and I went flying down the driveway for parts unknown. I never did find the hamburger.

When the car finally came to a halt, I was too stunned to move. Then this sweet, 81-year-old lady came hurrying up to my window to see if I was all right and begging me not to call the police. "I'm so sorry," she said. "I did this to someone else two weeks ago. Please don't report me! I'll fix your car."

I should have made a record of the accident, I know, but I just didn't have the heart. The lady in the tank and I were having approximately the same kind of month.

There are times such as this when it does feel like the cosmos is out to get you. I came across this B.C. cartoon a few years ago that sums up the way life can turn up the heat when we least expect it.

By permission of Johnny Hart and Creators Syndicate, Inc.

So life is a challenge. It was obviously designed to be that way. Look at how Jesus related to His disciples throughout His ministry on earth. He could hardly be accused of pampering these rugged men. Picture them in a small boat late one evening. You know the story. Jesus went to sleep on a cushion, and while He slept a "furious squall" came up. Remember that several of the disciples were professional fishermen and they knew very well what a storm can do to a small craft and its occupants. They were frightened—as you or I would have been. But there was the Master, unconcerned and uninvolved, sound asleep near the stern. Waves were crashing over the bow and threatening to sink the boat. The panic-stricken men could stand it no longer. They awakened Jesus and said, "Lord, save us! We're going to drown!" Before quieting the storm, He said to his disciples, "You of little faith, why are you so afraid?" (Matthew 8:23-26).

If I didn't know better, my sympathies would be with the disciples in this instance. Who could blame them for quaking in the path of the storm? There was no Coast Guard or helicopter service to pluck them out of the churning sea. If they ever fell overboard in this "furious squall" it would be curtains. Still, Jesus was disappointed by their panic. Why? Because fear and faith do not ride in the same boat. And because He wanted them to trust Him even when facing death. They would need that confidence in a few months!

Let's revisit Jesus and the disciples in yet another episode on the sea. According to Mark (6:45-50), He had instructed them to get in their boat and go on ahead of him to the city of Bethsaida. Then He went to a nearby mountainside to pray. Apparently, Jesus could see the entire lake from where He sat, and He observed that His disciples were "straining at the oars, because the wind was against them." The biblical account tells us, "About the fourth watch of the night he went out to them, walking on the lake" (v. 48). From the early evening to the fourth watch is a *seven-hour* passage of time. For seven hours, Jesus watched the disciples do battle with a severe head wind before He came to assist them. Yet they were in His vision and under His care throughout the night. Obviously, He permitted them to experience their need before coming to their rescue.

Sometimes He also lets you and me "struggle with the oars" until we recognize our dependence on Him. In so doing, He gives our faith an opportunity to grow and mature. But one thing is certain: We are ever in His vision. When His purposes are fulfilled and the time is right, He will calm the stormy sea and lead us to safety on the distant shore.

Let me take one more shot at the Christian writers and speakers who promote the expectation of ease in this Christian walk. They would have us believe that the followers of Jesus do not experience the trials and frustrations that pagans go through. Some of them appear so anxious to tell us what we want to hear that they distort the truths expressed in the Word. They would have us believe that the Lord rushes into action the instant we face a hardship, eliminating every discomfort or need. Well, sometimes He does just that. At other times He doesn't. Either way, He is there and has our lives in perfect control.

Let's look at another example of Jesus' relationship with his not-so-tough disciples. It occurred on the night before He was to be crucified. Peter, James, and John were with Him in the Garden of Gethsemane. As the night wore on, Jesus became overwhelmed with sorrow for what He was facing. He asked the three men to stay behind and keep watch while He went by Himself to pray. Three times during that hour He came back and found them asleep because "their eyes were heavy" (Matthew 26:43). As before, He expressed displeasure in their weakness.

We must remember that these men had also been under considerable stress in recent days. They understood they might be executed for their proximity to Jesus. That kind of danger causes fatigue—especially after being awake until the early morning hours. It was reasonable that the disciples would find it difficult to sit staring out into the night without lapsing into slumber. Yet Jesus expected them to stay awake, saying, "Watch and pray so that you will not fall into temptation. The spirit is willing, but the body is weak" (Matthew 26:41). There it is again. Jesus was urging His disciples to toughen up—to strive for greater control over their impulses. Why? Because weak flesh is more vulnerable to temptation.

Throughout Scripture we see this consistent pattern. The Lord wants His people to be strong. Read again the story of the children of Israel wandering around in the wilderness—lost, thirsty, dirty, and homeless. They became tired of eating the same monotonous food—manna—and longed for the familiar surroundings of Egypt. I might well have complained about every one of those frustrations if placed in a similar situation. But note what is written in Numbers 11:1:

> *Now the people complained about their hardships in the hearing of the Lord, and when he heard them his anger was aroused. Then fire from the Lord burned among them and consumed some of the outskirts of the camp.*

If that seems harsh, we must remember that God had chosen these people as His own, and He was doing a mighty work in their lives. He had rescued them from 400 years of Egyptian bondage. He even rolled back the Red Sea to facilitate their escape. He had cared for their every need, yet all they could do was grumble and complain. Scripture tells us God is long-suffering and slow to wrath—but He finally heard enough from this tribe of bellyachers.

Does that mean, as it would seem, that we should not feel free to express our deepest longings and frustrations to the Lord? Is He so demanding and detached that we must hide our fears from Him or try to be something we're not? Should we grin and bear it when every cell of our bodies aches in sorrow? Must we mimic ducks that sit quietly on a lake but are paddling like crazy below the surface? No! At least 100 Scriptures will refute that uncaring image of God. Jesus said, "Come to me, all you who are weary and burdened, and I will give you rest" (Matthew 11:28). We are told that He "knows how we are formed, he remembers that we are dust" (Psalm 103:14). He also understands that some of us are strong and confident by temperament. Others are naturally more anxious. That should come as no surprise to the One who made us the way we are.

I draw comfort, too, from God's compassion to David when he poured out his fears and frustrations. We have no record of the Lord's displeasure when David expressed his many sorrows and fears. What, then, was the difference between these acceptable "complaints" and those of the children of Israel many years before? The answer is seen in the nature of David's lamentations. They were expressed within a context of faith and dependence on God. Even when he was depressed, it is clear that he knew who his Lord was and where his allegiance rested. But the children of Israel were faithless and defiant in their grumbling. Once again, we see that everything in Scripture seems to reverberate to that vital little word, *faith*.

Let's summarize: We now know that faith must be tough, but why? Is there a logical reason why the Lord asks us to strengthen our resolve and meet our difficulties head-on? I believe it is because of the close interrelationship between mind, body, and spirit mentioned earlier. We cannot be spiritually stable and emotionally unstable at the same time. We are in a spiritual war with a deadly foe tracking us every hour of the day. We need to be in the best shape possible to cope with the darts and arrows he hurls our way. Flabby, overindulged, pampered Christians just don't have the stamina to fight this battle. Thus, the Lord puts us on a spiritual treadmill every now and then to keep us in good fighting condition.

It's the "adversity principle," and all of us are affected by it one way or the other.

8

FAITH
MUST BE
TOUGH

We ended the last chapter in a discussion about Christians being in proper "fighting condition." That analogy is not so farfetched. It is interesting that the Apostle Paul used military terminology to describe the service to which we are called. He wrote in 2 Timothy 2:3-4, "Endure hardship [there's that word again] with us like a good soldier of Christ Jesus. No one serving as a soldier gets involved in civilian affairs—he wants to please his commanding officer." That leads us to ask what this reference really means? How is the training of a soldier relevant to the life of a believer? And what does it mean to "endure hardship . . . like a good soldier"?

We have all seen John Wayne movies that made combat look like a romantic romp in the park. Men who have been through it tell a different story. The most graphic descriptions of battle I've read came from Bruce Catton's excellent books on the American Civil War. After reading several of these texts, I wrote the following description of military life in the nineteenth century and what soldiers endured during the War between the States. As you read it, reflect on Paul's analogy between good Christians and hardened troops:

> The Army of the Potomac *and other books by Catton provided a striking understanding of the toughness of both Yankees and Rebel soldiers. Their lives*

were filled with deprivation and danger that is hardly imaginable today. It was not unusual for the troops to make a two week forced march during which commanders would threaten the stragglers at swordpoint. They were often thrown into the heat of a terrible battle just moments after reaching the front. They would engage in exhausting combat for days, interspersed by sleepless nights on the ground—sometimes in freezing rain or snow. During the battle itself, they ate a dry, hard biscuit called hardtack, and very little else. In less combative times, they could add a little salt pork and coffee to their diet. That was it! As might be expected, their intestinal tracts were regularly shredded by diarrhea, dysentery and related diseases that decimated their ranks. The Union Army reported upwards of 200,000 casualties from disease, often disabling up to 50 percent of the soldiers. The Confederates suffered a similar fate.

Combat experience itself was unbelievably violent in those days. Thousands of men stood toe to toe and slaughtered one another like flies. After one particularly bloody battle in 1862, 5,000 men lay dead in an area of two square miles. 20,000 more were wounded. One witness said it was possible to walk on dead bodies for 100 yards without once stepping on the ground. Many of the wounded remained where they fell among dead men and horses for 12 or 14 hours, with their groans and cries echoing through the countryside.

Someone recently sent me a musket ball found on

an historic battlefield. I was surprised to see how large and heavy the molded lead was. It's no wonder limbs usually had to be amputated after being hit by these missiles. They tore into flesh and shattered bones beyond repair. Surgery was usually done without anesthetic, as unsterilized saws and knives were used to cut through flesh and bone. After each great battle, it was common for a huge mound of severed arms and legs to be piled up outside the surgeon's tent. Men were seen riding back from the front in wagons, holding bloody stumps upward to ease the pain. Antibiotics were nonexistent, and gangrene often finished the job a sharpshooter's bullet had begun.

While their willingness to endure these physical deprivations is impressive, one also has to admire the emotional toughness of the troops. They believed in their cause, whether Union or Confederate, and they committed their lives to it. Most believed that they would not survive the war, but that was of little consequence.

Please understand that I do not see unmitigated virtue in the heroic visions of that day. Indeed, men were all too willing to put their lives on the line for a war they poorly understood. But their dedication and personal sacrifice remain today as memorials to their time.

There is, perhaps, no better illustration of this commitment to principle and honor than is seen in a letter written by Major Sullivan Ballou of the Union army. He penned it to his wife, Sarah, on July 14, 1861, one week before the Battle of Bull Run. They had been married only six years. These powerful words still touch my soul:

My Very Dear Sarah:

The indications are very strong that we shall move in a few days—perhaps tomorrow. Lest I should not be able to write again, I feel impelled to write a few lines that may fall under your eye when I shall be no more. . . .

I have no misgivings about or lack of confidence in the cause in which I am engaged, and my courage does not halt or falter. I know how strongly American civilization now leans on the triumph of the Government, and how great a debt we owe to those who went before us through the blood and suffering of the Revolution. And I am willing, perfectly willing to lay down all my joys in this life to help maintain this Government and to pay that debt. . . .

Sarah, my love for you is deathless: it seems to bind me with mighty cables that nothing but Omnipotence could break, and yet my love of country comes over me like a strong wind, and bears me irresistibly on, with all these chains, to the battlefield.

The memories of all the blissful moments I have spent with you come creeping over me, and I feel most deeply grateful to God, and you, that I have enjoyed them so long. And how hard it is for me to give them up, and burn to ashes the hopes of future years, when, God willing, we might still have lived and loved together and seen our sons grown up to honorable manhood around us.

If I do not [return], my dear Sarah, never forget how much I love you, and when my last breath escapes me on the battle-field, it will whisper your name. Forgive my many faults and the many pains I have caused you. How thoughtless, how foolish I have often-times been. . . .

O Sarah, if the dead can come back to this earth, and flit unseen around those they loved, I shall always be near you in the gladdest day, and in the darkest night, amidst your happiest scenes and gloomiest hours—always, always: and if there be a soft breeze upon your cheek, it shall be my breath: or the cool air cools your throbbing temple, it shall be my spirit passing by.

Sarah, do not mourn me dead: think I am gone, and wait for me, for we shall meet again. . . .
Sullivan[1]

Major Ballou was killed one week later at the first battle of Bull Run. I wonder, don't you, if he did indeed utter Sarah's name as he lay dying on the battlefield.

1 Adin Ballou, compiler and editor, *History and Genealogy of the Ballous in America* (Providence, R.I.: E. L. Freeman & Sons, 1888), pp. 1058-1059.

She undoubtedly suffered the greater pain in the aftermath of that terrible war.

Is this the level of dedication and sacrifice to which the Apostle Paul calls us in 2 Timothy 2? I believe it is, yet the concept seems almost unreasonable in this day of individual rights and self-fulfillment. How long has it been since we've thought of ourselves as highly disciplined soldiers in the army of the Lord? That was a familiar theme in years past. "Onward, Christian Soldiers" was one of the favorite songs of the church. Christians, it proclaimed, were "marching as to war, with the cross of Jesus going on before." We also sang, "Stand up! Stand up for Jesus, ye soldiers of the cross." Then there was "Dare to be a Daniel, dare to stand alone. Dare to have a purpose firm, dare to make it known." That was the way Christians saw their responsibility in days past. Well, we've come a long way, baby. Now our emphasis is on harnessing the power of God for more successful (and prosperous) living. Something seems to have been lost in the translation!

One of the popular choruses of today offers this happy thought, "Something good is going to happen today, happen today, happen today. Something good is going to happen today, Jesus of Nazareth is passing this way." I have a strong dislike for that well-intentioned little rendition because it is based on bad theology. I understand how the lyrics are intended to be interpreted, but they imply that Christianity guarantees a person only "good things." It is not true. Let's be honest. As the world interprets it, something terrible could happen to you today. Christians do get sick and die, just like the rest of the world. They do lose their jobs like other people, and they do have car wrecks and dental problems and sick kids. Believing otherwise is a trap from which many young believers, and some old ones, never escape!

There is a reason why the great hymns of the church have endured, in some cases for hundreds of years. They are based not on words that tickle our ears, but on solid theological truth. One of my favorites relating to our theme is entitled "Jesus, I My Cross Have Taken." The lyrics were written by Henry F. Lyte back in 1824, and the music was arranged from Mozart. Absorb, if you will, the truth in these incredible words,

Jesus, I my cross have taken,
All to leave and follow Thee;
Naked, poor, despised, forsaken,
Thou from hence my all shalt be:
Perish every fond ambition,
All I've sought, and hoped, and known;
Yet how rich is my condition—
God and heaven are still my own!

Go, then, earthly fame and treasure!
Come, disaster, scorn and pain!
In Thy service, pain is pleasure;
With Thy favor, loss is gain
I have called Thee, "Abba, Father";
I have stayed my heart on Thee

Storms may howl, and clouds may gather;
All must work for good to me.

This message is a little different from "Something gooooood is going to happen today," and it may even be unpalatable to a modern world. But it is biblically accurate, and you can build a rock-solid foundation of faith on it. With it, you can cope with whatever life throws at you, even when God makes absolutely no sense. It will hold you when you walk through the valley of the shadow of death, because you need fear no evil. Life can never take you by surprise, again. Everything is committed to Him, whether you understand the circumstances or not. He becomes your possessor and your dispossessor. With this biblical understanding and a tough, well-fortified faith, the "awesome why" loses its scary significance. A better question becomes "Why does it matter?" It is not your responsibility to explain what God is doing with your life. He has not provided enough information to figure it out. Instead, you are asked to turn loose and let God be God. Therein lies the secret to the "peace that transcends understanding."

This theological interpretation may not be what the reader wanted to hear—especially the one who has grieved until there are no more tears to shed. If you are that person, I hope you will understand that I have not intended to trivialize your loss. My heart is tender toward those who have undergone severe suffering. Just last week I received a letter from a father whose daughter was killed in a car crash some 18 months ago. He wrote to say how keenly he and his wife still feel the pain—pain that few of his fellow believers seem to comprehend. As I read his words and thought of my own daughter who is just a few years older, I grieved with this heartsick father. Life can be incredibly cruel to those who have loved and lost. Such a person needs the loving friendship and prayers of a Christian brother or sister who will simply be there to say "I care." More importantly, he needs to know God cares!

I am convinced that the heart of the Lord is drawn to those who hold fast to their faith in such times of despair. How tenderly he must look upon those who have lost a beloved son or daughter. What compassion He feels for those with lifelong physical deformities and diseases. This identification with the woes of mankind is a major theme of Scripture.

I think often of a young man in his early teens whom Dr. Tony Campolo described in one of his messages. This boy was named Jerry, and he had been afflicted from birth with cerebral palsy. Jerry walked and talked with great difficulty, yet he came to a Christian summer camp where Dr. Campolo was the principal speaker. It was apparent from the first day that Jerry would be rejected by the other junior highers who immediately set about establishing a hierarchy of social power. An "in group" emerged, as it always does, composed mostly of the good-looking guys and the cute girls. They were far too sophisticated and selfish to mess around with a cripple—a loser like Jerry. They were also rude to the other outcasts—the kids who had been hurt and those who lacked confidence. They didn't stand a chance.

All week Dr. Campolo watched Jerry struggle to find his place. It was brutal to witness. The popular kids mocked the way he walked and talked. They would imitate his labored speech, saying "Whhaaaaaaaat . . . tiiiimmmme . . . issssssss . . . ccrrrraaaaaffffttttss . . . cclllaaaaasssss?" Then they would all laugh hysterically as though Jerry were deaf. At other times, they avoided him like a plague. Dr. Campolo said he has never hated anyone in his life, but he came close to it in that instance—seeing what those insensitive and cruel teenagers were doing to the spirit of one who had already suffered more than his share.

A service was held on the final morning of the camp, during which the students were invited to give their testimonies about what Jesus Christ had meant to them. One by one, the superstars came to the microphone—the athletes, the cheerleaders, and the popular kids. They delivered their little canned speeches, but there was no power in their witness. Their words were empty.

Then, as Dr. Campolo sat on the platform, he was startled to see Jerry making his way down the aisle from the back of the auditorium. The other students saw him too, and they began to whisper and point. Then a ripple of laughter passed over the crowd. Ever so slowly, Jerry came to the platform and then carefully and painfully climbed the three stairs at the side. Finally, he reached the microphone. He stood for a moment looking at his peers, and then said with great effort, "I . . . loooooovvvvve . . . Jeeeeessssuuuusss . . . aaannnnndddddddddd . . . Jeeeeeessssuuusssss . . . looooooovvvvvvessssss . . . mmeeeeeeeeeeee." Then Jerry turned to make his long journey back to his seat.

Campolo said Jerry's simple testimony went through that crowd of teenagers like a bolt of lightning. His expression of love for God, despite the physical disability and the ridicule he had taken, exposed the sin and selfishness in their lives. They began streaming into the aisles and down to a place of prayer at the front. The Lord had used the least capable spokesman among all those teenagers to accomplish His purposes. Why? Because Jerry was tough enough to be His vessel.

Just how tough is your faith? How secure is mine? Will we permit the Lord to use our weakness, our disability, our disappointment, our inadequacy, to accomplish His purposes? Will you and I, like Jerry, worship and serve this Master even in suffering? Does our "expectation" as followers of Jesus leave room for frustration and imperfection? Does the Word have anything to say to us here about how we live our lives and what causes us to complain? It certainly does!

My favorite Scripture specifically addresses this issue of toughness, and we will conclude with its powerful insight. The passage is found in a letter to the Philippians, which was written by the Apostle Paul from Rome, where he was confined and may eventually have been executed for sharing his faith in Jesus Christ. Paul had every right to be distraught at that stage of his life. What had happened to him was not fair! There had been times recently when he had been publicly whipped; he had gone without adequate food and clothing; he was once stoned and left for dead. He could have complained bitterly that the Lord had called him to a difficult task and then virtually abandoned him. The "awesome why" could certainly have been on his lips. But that was *not* what Paul was thinking.

He wrote to the believers at Philippi:

> *Rejoice in the Lord always. I will say it again: Rejoice! Let your gentleness be evident to all. The Lord is near. Do not be anxious about anything, but in everything, by prayer and petition, with thanksgiving, present your requests to God. And the peace of God, which transcends all understanding, will guard your hearts and your minds in Christ Jesus. (Philippians 4:4-7)*

Then Paul addressed the matter of expectations directly:

> *I know what it is to be in need, and I know what it is to have plenty. I have learned the secret of being content in any and every situation, whether well fed or hungry, whether living in plenty or in want. I can do everything through him who gives me strength. (Philippians 4:12-13)*

Paul's secret of contentment emerges from a universal principle of human nature. It is to trust God regardless of the circumstances and not to expect too much perfection in this life. A better day is coming for those whose source of contentment is in the personhood of Christ Jesus!

9

THE
WAGES
OF
SIN

We have been discussing those occasions when hardship and difficulty come sweeping into our lives for no apparent reason. Accidents, death, sickness, earthquakes, fires, violence, etc., naturally lead the survivors to ask, "What did we do to deserve *this?*" Their inability to link these inexplicable "acts of God" with their own misbehavior often creates a sense of betrayal and victimization. It just doesn't seem fair.

There is another source of pain and suffering in our lives, however, that must be considered. It was described by Dr. Karl Menninger in his book *Whatever Became of Sin?* He wrote about the almost-forgotten concept of disobedience to God and how it undermines our well-being. Indeed, much of the heartache for which God is often blamed results from old-fashioned sin. I'm referring not to the curse of Adam's sin, but to specific sinful behavior that wreaks havoc in the human family.

Scripture makes it clear that there is a direct link between disobedience to God and the consequence of death. James describes the connection this way: "Each one is tempted when, by his own evil desire, he is dragged away and enticed. Then, after desire has conceived, it gives birth to sin; and sin, when it is full-grown, gives birth to death" (James 1:14-15).

All sin bears that deadly characteristic. It's not that

God sits in His heaven and determines to abuse those who make mistakes. But He forbade certain behavior because He knew it would ultimately destroy its victims. It is not God who leads to death, but sin. And sin becomes a cancer that consumes those who embrace it.

The Apostle Paul used these words to describe the malignant nature of sin in his own life and the wonderful remedy available to the believer: "What a wretched man I am! Who will rescue me from this body of death? Thanks be to God—[it is done] through Jesus Christ our Lord!" (Romans 7:24-25).

What is the "body of death" to which Paul referred? This term described a horrible method of execution used by the Romans in those days. A cadaver would be attached to a condemned person in such a way that he could not extricate himself from it. Then the rotting flesh of the carcass would begin to pollute the body of the prisoner. Inevitably, terrible diseases and infections would lead to a slow and painful death. This, said Paul, is what sin does to an unregenerate person. It attaches itself to its victim and pollutes everything it touches. Without the cleansing blood of Jesus Christ, all of us are hopelessly condemned by this plague of wickedness.

This link between sin and death applies not only to individuals, but to nations as well. During the eighteenth century, for example, American plantation owners and businessmen embraced slavery as a source of cheap and convenient labor. Surely they knew it was an evil proposition right from the beginning. Slave traders abducted peaceful African villagers and hauled them off in chains.

They were packed so tightly on filthy, disease-infested ships that up to 50 percent died en route to this country. Every one of those deaths constituted a murder, yet there was a willing market in America for the survivors. They were bought and sold like animals, without regard to family integrity. Children were taken from parents and husbands were separated from wives. Some were beaten, some were raped, and some were worked to death. The entire system was reprehensible, yet it was embraced by a society that professed to be God-fearing. The seeds of destruction were planted.

When sin is full grown, said James, it brings forth death. Alas, the terrible sin of slavery reached its full maturity in 1860 when it contributed to a shameful and devastating Civil War. An entire nation was soon bathed in its own blood. More Americans were killed in that struggle than in all our other conflicts combined, including the Revolution, World Wars I and II, Korea, Vietnam, and every skirmish in between. Indeed, 600,000 husbands, fathers, and sons paid the supreme price for the folly of a nation's greed and exploitation.

Now here we go again. Nearly 30 million unborn babies have been killed since the Supreme Court issued its despicable *Roe v. Wade* decision in 1973. That number represents more than 10 percent of the U.S. population, and it is growing by 4,110 per day. Such bloodshed and butchery, now occurring worldwide, is unprecedented in human history, yet we've only seen the beginning. Don't tell me this crime against humanity will go unpunished! Those voiceless little people cry out to the Almighty from the incinerators and the garbage heaps where they have been discarded. Someday, this "unborn holocaust" will rain death and destruction upon our nation. Just wait. You'll see. It is in the nature of the universe. Sin inevitably devastates a people who embrace it.

Read the words of the Lord spoken to the children of Israel almost 4,000 years ago: "This day I call heaven and earth as witnesses against you that I have set before you life and death, blessings and curses. Now choose life, so that you and your children may live" (Deuteronomy 30:19). Alas, we have chosen death! And we will have hell to pay for it.

Permit me another example. There has been a general understanding for thousands of years that premarital and extramarital sexual behavior is dangerous. Those who broke the rules put themselves at risk for syphilis, gonorrhea, unwanted pregnancy, and social rejection. Women, even more than men, understood the dangers of promiscuity and tried to protect themselves from it. There were exceptions, of course, but the culture generally recognized and supported Christian standards of morality. And you can be sure that those principles were passionately defended on behalf of the nation's teenagers. As late as 1956, Elvis Presley's suggestive hip movements on stage, which are tame by today's standards, produced a storm of protest from parents. They understood where that road would lead.

This commitment to premarital chastity and marital

fidelity was widely supported in our society from 1620 to 1967. Then, suddenly, adherence to the biblical standard disintegrated. It has been said that never in history has a culture rejected its primary system of values more quickly than in the late sixties. Promiscuous behavior became known as "the new morality," which was neither new nor moral. But it was fun. And it became almost a cause célèbre. Indeed, there was a striking defiance of convention and tradition among the young of that day. They've paid a fine price for it.

The tragic thing about the sudden crumbling of sexual mores in the late sixties and early seventies was the waffling of the mainline Protestant church. At a time when Christians should have risen to defend biblical morality, many denominations were having their own doubts about its validity. A great internal debate raged about whether or not the old prohibitions still made sense. That period in church history was reported in an article entitled "The New Commandment: Thou Shalt Not—Maybe" in *Time* magazine (December 13, 1971):

> On Mount Sinai, God was unequivocal: "Thou shalt not commit adultery." Traditionally, most devout Christians have interpreted the Hebraic commandment to extend to all sexual relations outside marriage. Jesus even condemned lustful thoughts, saying that the man who indulged them had "already committed adultery in his heart." But in recent years, pressed both by changing sexual behavior and by liberal theologians, the churches have reluctantly

come to grips with a "new morality" that questions whether any "sin"—including adultery or other nonmarital sex—is wrong in all circumstances.

The movement began in the 1960s with a group of writers who championed "contextual" or "situation" ethics. As defined in a widely read book by Episcopalian Joseph Fletcher, situation ethics holds that there are always circumstances in which absolute principles of behavior break down. The only valid ethical test, the argument goes, is what God's love demands in each particular situation.

The article went on to describe four mainline denominations that were undergoing efforts to loosen standards of sexual behavior for their members. Each had received reports from prestigious internal committees that had recommended a redefinition of immoral conduct. One of the larger churches was considering a resolution that specifically condoned sexual intercourse for unmarried people, homosexuals, and those living in "other" styles of interpersonal relationship. Another denomination weighed a report that indicated premarital sexual behavior was not intrinsically wrong unless it was selfish and exploitative in nature. Another was considering a recommended "sliding scale of allowable premarital sex, geared to the permanence, depth, and maturity of the relationship." This report also described "exceptional circumstances" in which adultery might be justified. The fourth denomination had received a statement written by six Christian education executives who maintained that "sex is moral if the partners are committed to the 'fulfilling of each other's personhood'—pointedly omitting marriage as a prerequisite."

The *Time* article ended with this statement:

> *Against the traditional concept that God wants men to conform to a fixed divine design, the new morality stakes its case on the idea that God would prefer men to make their own responsible decisions.*

What a perversion of the biblical standard! Nowhere in Scripture—not once in 66 books—is there the slightest indication that God wants us to make up our own rules. Yet that was the tenor of the times.

Now, more than two decades later, we find that the radical ideas being introduced in 1971 are widely adopted in society. The old morality has been severely weakened, and in its place has come a freer standard of behavior. Some churches have gone on to endorse homosexual life-styles and even, in a few cases, the ordination of homosexual and lesbian ministers. Teenagers, even in conservative churches, are only slightly less "sexually active" than those who are unchurched. America and most Western nations have successfully thrown off the shackles of legalism. A new day has dawned! But before our celebration hits a fever pitch, it seems appropriate that we ask how the "new morality" has worked out so far. What has been the consequence of the revisionism that was debated so vigorously in the early 1970s?

Well, you know the answer to that question. The cancer of sin has matured and is yielding a staggering harvest of death. Read the statistics—and weep:

- *One million Americans are infected with HIV (and 110 million worldwide).[1] Every one of these unfortunate people will die of AIDS eventually, barring the improbable development of a cure.*

- *One million new cases of pelvic inflammatory disease occur annually.[2]*

- *1.3 million new cases of gonorrhea occur annually.[3] New strains have developed resistance to penicillin.*

- *Syphilis is at a 40-year high, with 134,000 new infections per year.[4]*

- *500,000 new cases of herpes occur annually.[5] It is estimated that 16.4 percent of the U. S. population ages 15–74 is infected, totaling more than 25 million Americans—among certain groups, the infection rate is as high as 60 percent.[6]*

1 Pamela McDonnell, Sexually Transmitted Diseases Division, Centers for Disease Control, U.S. Dept. of Health & Human Services, telephone interview, March 16, 1992.

2 *Ibid.*, March 18, 1992

3 STD, CDC, *HIV Prevention*, p. 13..

4 *Ibid.*

5 *Ibid.*

6 Robert E. Johnson, et al, "A Seroepidemiologic Survey of the Prevalence of Herpes Simplex Virus Type 2 Infection in the United States," *New England Journal of Medicine* 321 (July 6, 1989): 7-12.

- *The most common killer of women among the sexually transmitted diseases is not AIDS, as is widely believed.[7] It is the human papilloma virus (HPV), which can cause cancer of the cervix. 6,000 women die of this disease each year in the United States. 24 million American women are now infected with HPV.[8]*

- *One and a half million unborn babies are aborted each year.[9]*

- *Up to 20 percent of brides are pregnant at the altar.[10]*

- *The divorce rate in America is the highest in the civilized world.[11]*

We are a sick people with weak, ineffectual families. The United States Centers for Disease Control reported recently that 43 million of our citizens (nearly one in five) are infected with an incurable sexually transmitted virus. Some will die of it. Others will suffer for the rest of their lives. Can anyone doubt that sexual liberation has been a social, spiritual, and physiological disaster!?

It should have been anticipated. Mankind has been

7 Joseph S. McIlhaney, Jr., M.D., *Sexuality and Sexually Transmitted Diseases* (Grand Rapids: Baker, 1990), p. 137.
8 Kay Stone, Sexually Transmitted Diseases Division, Centers for Disease Control, U.S. Dept. of Health & Human Services, telephone interview, March 20, 1992.
9 U.S. Bureau of the Census, *Statistical Abstract of the United States: 1991,* 111th ed. (Washington, D.C., 1991), p. 71.
10 Patricia McLaughlin, "Wedding Symbolism," *St. Petersburg Times* (June 2, 1990): p. 1D, citing unpublished data from the National Center for Health Statistics.
11 1990 *Demographic Yearbook,* 42nd Issue (New York: United Nations, 1992), p. 752.

trying to sin with impunity ever since the serpent tempted Eve in the Garden of Eden. He told her, "You shall *not* surely die." He lied. The deception continues today. Sex educators and Planned Parenthood types are still telling our kids they can beat the system by the use of condoms. Alas, the federal government has spent 2 billion dollars to promote the notion that premarital sex is fine for those who simply "do it right." But their program has failed miserably. Why? Because the moral foundation of the universe is an expression of God's own nature, and *everything* is governed by it. Those who attempt to sin without consequences are destined to fall on their faces!

I sometimes ask people if they can remember the first thing created by God when He set the worlds in place. They try to recall from Genesis 1 whether He first made light, the firmament, or the heavens. None of those answers is correct. We find in Proverbs 8 that the creation of the physical universe was preceded by something else. In this passage, God's value system—His "wisdom"—speaks in first person. Let's read it together:

> *The Lord brought me [wisdom] forth as the first of his works, before his deeds of old; I was appointed from eternity, from the beginning, before the world began. When there were no oceans, I was given birth, when there were no springs abounding with water; before the mountains were settled in place, before the hills, I was given birth, before he made the earth*

or its fields or any of the dust of the world. I was there when he set the heavens in place, when he marked out the horizon on the face of the deep, when he established the clouds above and fixed securely the fountains of the deep, when he gave the sea its boundary so the waters would not overstep his command, and when he marked out the foundations of the earth. Then I was the craftsman at his side. I was filled with delight day after day, rejoicing always in his presence, rejoicing in his whole world and delighting in mankind. "Now then, my sons, listen to me; blessed are those who keep my ways. Listen to my instruction and be wise; do not ignore it. Blessed is the man who listens to me, watching daily at my doors, waiting at my doorway. For whoever finds me finds life and receives favor from the Lord. But whoever fails to find me harms himself; all who hate me love death." (Proverbs 8:22-36)

What a clear statement of the divine nature! The moral foundation for the universe was not an afterthought that came along when mankind was created. The Ten Commandments did not occur to the Lord after He witnessed the children of Israel's disobedience in the wilderness. No, the meaning of right and wrong emanated from God's own character, and it has always existed. Certainly, it predated the work of creation described in Genesis 1.

What does this mean for you and me? It illustrates the authority behind the moral laws found in Scripture!

They actually outrank the physical laws in significance. In fact, the physical universe will someday pass away and be replaced, but God's moral nature is eternal. And anyone who opposes it "love[s] death."

Now, why have I offered this explanation in a discussion about God's intervention in our lives? Because I believe many of the trials and tribulations that come our way are of our own making. Some are the direct consequence of sin, as we have seen. In other cases, the pain we experience is a result of unwise decisions. We make such a mess of our lives by foolishness and irresponsibility. When one considers the range of sheer nonsense that human beings can generate, it is understandable why author Mark Twain once said, "At times it does seem a shame that Noah and his party didn't miss the boat."

I'm reminded of a deep-sea fishing trip I took with my son, Ryan, when he was about 10 years old. The captain of our boat located a huge school of albacore, which sent 25 weekend fishermen into a frenzy of hyperventilation. We began pulling in fish like crazy. I was so busy with a tuna of my own that I failed to notice what my inexperienced son was doing. Then I looked down at him and saw that he was up to his elbows in a record-breaking backlash. I still can't imagine how that kid could get a perfectly spooled reel of line so thoroughly tangled. It was a hopeless case. Houdini himself couldn't have unraveled it. I had to cut and discard about 150 yards of what Ryan called "string" to get him straightened out.

His knotted, twisted line is symbolic of what many of us do with our lives. We drink too much or gamble compulsively or allow pornography to possess our minds. We drive too fast and work like there's no tomorrow. We challenge the boss disrespectfully and then blow up when he strikes back. We spend money we don't have and can't possibly repay. We fuss and fight at home and create misery for ourselves and our families. We not only borrow trouble—we go looking for it. We toy with the dragon of infidelity. We break the laws of God and then honestly believe we have beaten the odds. Then when the "wages" of those sins and foolishness come due, we turn our shocked faces up to heaven and cry, "Why me, Lord?" In truth, we are suffering the natural consequences of dangerous behavior that is guaranteed to produce pain.

I would not imply that every physical illness or heartache is the result of sin, of course, and we discussed that trap in chapter 5. There are situations, however, where the connection is undeniable. I think of sickness that emanates from abuse of one's body, such as lung cancer resulting from cigarette smoke, or cirrhosis caused by alcoholism, or mental illness precipitated by narcotics usage. These are self-inflicted wounds.

A more relevant example today is the HIV phenomenon. The question is often raised, Has God sent the AIDS epidemic as a punishment for homosexual behavior? I believe emphatically that the correct answer is no! Many innocent victims, including newborn babies, are suffering and dying from the disease. A curse from God would be more specific to the perpetrator. However, the HIV infection is *spread* by sodomy, drug usage, and promiscuity, so sinful behavior has helped to create the epidemic that now threatens the human family.

Think of it this way. If I choose to leap off a 10-story building, I will die when my body hits the ground below. It's inevitable. But gravity was not designed by God to punish my misbehavior. He established physical laws that can't be violated without great peril. So it is with His moral laws. They are as real and predictable as the principles that govern the physical universe. Thus, He knew (and we should have known) with the onset of the sexual revolution back in 1967 that this day of disease and promiscuity would come. It is here, and what we do with our situation will determine how much we and our children will suffer in the future.

Perhaps a concluding story will help us wrap up this discussion and illustrate where I believe we are headed in the struggle between good and evil.

I heard about a missionary in Africa who returned to his hut late one afternoon. As he entered the front door he was confronted by a huge python on the floor. He ran back to his truck and retrieved a .45-caliber pistol. Unfortunately, he had only one bullet in the chamber and no extra ammunition. Taking careful aim, the missionary sent that single shot into the head of the reptile. The snake was mortally wounded, but it did not die quickly. It began frantically thrashing and writhing on the floor. Retreating to the front yard, the missionary could hear furniture breaking and lamps crashing. Finally, all was quiet, and the man cautiously reentered his house. He found the snake dead, but the entire interior of the hut was shattered. In its dying moments, the python had unleashed all its mighty power and wrath on everything in sight.

Later, the missionary drew an analogy between the python and the great serpent named Satan. Our adversary has already been mortally wounded by the death and resurrection of Jesus Christ. (In Genesis 3:15 the Lord said to the serpent, "And I will put enmity between you and the woman, and between your offspring and hers; he will crush your head, and you will strike his heel.") Thus, the serpent's days are numbered and he knows it. In a final desperate effort to thwart the will of God and deceive His people, Satan has unleashed all his fury. He is fostering hate and deceit and aggression wherever human interests collide. He especially despises the institution of the family, which is symbolic of the relationship between Jesus Christ and His church.

How can we survive in such a dangerous environment? How can we cope with the fury of Satan in his final days? Admittedly, we would stand no chance in our own strength. But listen to what Jesus said about His followers: "My sheep listen to my voice; I know them, and they follow me. I give them eternal life, and they shall never perish; *no one can snatch them out of my hand*. My Father, who has given them to me, is greater than all" (John 10:27-29).

Because of the Redeemer, we need not fear the great

deceiver—the father of lies. We are promised throughout Scripture that we are never left to fight our battles alone. John, the disciple whom Jesus loved, penned these words of encouragement after a lifetime of service to his Master: "My dear children, I write this to you so that you will not sin. But if anybody does sin, we have one who speaks to the Father in our defense—Jesus Christ, the Righteous One. He is the atoning sacrifice for our sins, and not only for ours but also for the sins of the whole world" (1 John 2:1-2).

The Apostle Paul confirmed that sin need not hold power over us. He wrote:

> *So now, since we have been made right in God's sight by faith in his promises, we can have real peace with him because of what Jesus Christ our Lord has done for us. For because of our faith, he has brought us into this place of highest privilege where we now stand, and we confidently and joyfully look forward to actually becoming all that God has in mind for us to be. (Romans 5:1-2, TLB)*

That is great news for all who are weary and burdened by the stresses of living. It all comes down to this simple concept: God is not against us for our sins. He is *for* us against our sins. That makes all the difference.

10

MORE QUESTIONS AND ANSWERS

Let's return now to a discussion format, focusing on some additional issues we have introduced.

Q1. **Our three children were prayed for before they were conceived, and we have held their names before the Lord almost every day of their lives. Yet our middle daughter has chosen to reject our faith and do things she knows are wrong. She's living with a twice-divorced man and apparently has no intention of marrying him. She has had at least two abortions that we know about, and her language is disgraceful. My wife and I have prayed until we're exhausted, and yet she has shown no interest in returning to the church. At times, I become very angry at God for allowing this terrible thing to happen. I have wept until there are just no more tears. Can you offer us any encouragement?**

A1. I can certainly understand your pain. It is my belief that more people have become disillusioned with God over the waywardness of a son or daughter than any other issue. There is *nothing* more important to most Christian parents than the salvation of their children. Every other goal and achievement in life is anemic and insignificant compared to this transmission of faith to their offspring. That is the only way they can be together throughout eternity, and they, like you, have been praying day and night for spiritual awakening. Unfortunately, if God does not answer those prayers quickly, there is a tendency to blame Him and to struggle with intense feelings of bitterness. The "betrayal barrier" claims another victim!

Often, this anger at the Lord results from a misunderstanding of what He will and won't do in the lives of those for whom we intercede. The key question is this: Will God require our offspring to serve Him if they choose a path of rebellion? It is a critically important question.

The answer, according to Dr. John White and the theologians with whom I have spoken, is that God will not force Himself on anyone. If that was His inclination, no person would ever be lost. Second Peter 3:9 says, "He is patient with you, not wanting *anyone* to perish, but *everyone* to come to repentance." To claim this great salvation, there is a condition. An individual must reach out and take it. He or she must repent of sins and believe on the name of the Lord Jesus Christ. Without that step of faith, the gift of forgiveness and eternal life is impossible.

What does prayer accomplish, then, if there is a realm into which the Father will not intrude? Quoting Dr. White's insightful book *Parents in Pain*:

> *Here lies a key to understanding how we may pray for our own children or for anyone else. We may*

ask with every confidence that God will open the eyes of the morally and spiritually blind. We may ask that the self-deceptions which sinners hide behind may be burned away in the fierce light of truth, that dark caverns may be rent asunder to let the sunlight pour in, that self-disguises may be stripped from a man or woman to reveal the horror of their nakedness in the holy light of God. We may ask above all that the glory of the face of Christ will shine through the spiritual blindness caused by the god of this world (2 Corinthians 4:4). All of this we can ask with every assurance that God will not only hear but will delight to answer.

But we may not ask him to force a man, woman, or child to love and trust him. To deliver them from overwhelming temptation: yes. To give them every opportunity: yes. To reveal his beauty, his tenderness, his forgiveness: yes. But to force a man against his will to bow the knee: not in this life. And to force a man to trust him: never.[1]

Said another way, the Lord will not save a person against his will, but He has a thousand ways of making him more willing. Our prayers unleash the power of God in the life of another individual. We have been granted the privilege of entering into intercessory prayer for our loved ones and of holding their names and faces before the Father. In return, He makes the

---

1 John White, *Parents in Pain* (Downers Grove, Ill.: InterVarsity Press, 1979), pp. 47-48.

all-important choices crystal clear to that individual and brings positive influences into his or her life to maximize the probability of doing what is right. Beyond that, He will not go.

Admittedly, we have strolled into deep theological water here. Who knows exactly how God responds to intercessory prayer and how He deals with a wayward heart? How can I explain the prayers of my great-grandfather (on my mother's side), who died the year before I was born? This wonderful man of God, G. W. McCluskey, took it upon himself to spend the hour between 11:00 A.M. and 12:00 noon every day in prayer specifically for the spiritual welfare of his family. He was talking to the Lord not only about those loved ones who were then alive. McCluskey was also praying for generations not yet born. This good man was talking to the Lord about me, even before I was conceived.

Toward the end of his life, my great-grandfather made a startling announcement. He said God had promised him that every member of four generations—both those living and those not yet born—would be believers. Well, I represent the fourth generation down from his own, and it has worked out more interestingly than even he might have assumed.

The McCluskeys had two girls, one of whom was my grandmother and the other, my great-aunt. Both grew up and married ministers in the denomination of their father and mother. Between these women, five girls and one boy were born. One of them was my mother. All five of the girls married ministers in the denomination of their grandfather, and the boy became one. That brought it down to my generation. My cousin H. B. London and I were the first to go through college, and we were roommates. In the beginning of our sophomore year, he announced that God was calling him to preach. And I can assure you, I began to get very nervous about the family tradition!

I never felt God was asking me to be a minister, so I went to graduate school and became a psychologist. And yet, I have spent my professional life speaking, teaching, and writing about the importance of my faith in Jesus Christ. At times as I sit on a platform waiting to address a church filled with Christians, I wonder if my great-grandfather isn't smiling at me from somewhere. His prayers have reached across four generations of time to influence what I am doing with my life today.

What does that say about free moral agency and the right to choose? I don't have a clue. I only know that God honors the prayers of His righteous followers, and we should stay on our faces before Him until each child has been granted every opportunity to repent. We must remember, however, that God will not ride roughshod over the will of any individual. He deals respectfully with each person and seeks to attract him or her to Himself. It is wrong, therefore, to blame God if that process takes years to accomplish—or even if it never comes to pass. That is the price of freedom.

Q2. (Follow-up question) Your answer implies that we should continue to pray for our daughter

**year after year until she comes back to her faith.
Does that mean that God will not be offended by
our asking Him repeatedly for the same request?
Is that what He wants of us on her behalf?**

A2. Yes. If what you are requesting is undeniably
in the will of God, such as praying for the salvation
of your daughter, I think you should keep the matter
before Him until you receive the answer. There is a
continuing spiritual battle under way for her soul,
and your prayers are vital in winning that struggle.
Paul admonished us to "pray without ceasing"
(1 Thessalonians 5:17, NKJV). Isn't that what Jesus
was teaching in the parable of the Unjust Judge? Let's
read it in the Book of Luke:

> *Then Jesus told his disciples a parable to show them
> that they should always pray and not give up. He
> said: "In a certain town there was a judge who
> neither feared God nor cared about men. And
> there was a widow in that town who kept coming to
> him with the plea, 'Grant me justice against my
> adversary.'*
>
> *"For some time he refused. But finally he said to
> himself, 'Even though I don't fear God or care
> about men, yet because this widow keeps bothering
> me, I will see that she gets justice, so that she won't
> eventually wear me out with her coming!'"*
>
> *And the Lord said, "Listen to what the unjust
> judge says. And will not God bring about justice*

*for his chosen ones, who cry out to him day and
night? Will he keep putting them off? I tell you, he
will see that they get justice, and quickly." (Luke
18:1-8)*

I love that Scripture because it tells us that God is not
irritated by our persistence in prayer. He urges us not
to give up, but to bombard heaven with the desires of
our hearts. That is encouragement enough to keep me
praying for a lifetime.

I shared a story earlier about my great-grandfather on
my mother's side of the family. With your indulgence,
let me relate an incident from the life of my paternal
grandmother, Juanita Dobson. She understood what it
meant to "pray without ceasing," even when there was
little evidence to encourage her. She was a deeply
committed Christian who was married to an independent, nonbelieving husband. Because he was a
moral and decent man, he saw no need for a personal
relationship with Jesus Christ. That fact nearly damned
him.

He didn't mind his wife going to church and doing
her religious thing, but he would have no part in it. He
especially resented any effort to drag him into it. That
door was slammed shut. Instead of trying to goad her
husband into a Christian commitment, therefore, Juanita began a campaign of prayer on his behalf that
continued for decades. She fasted for his salvation
regularly for years, despite the lack of evidence that her
petitions were even being heard!

Still, my grandfather's heart remained hard and cold. But when he was 69 years old, he suffered a series of strokes that left him partially paralyzed. He had been a powerful man, a six-foot-four-inch railroad conductor, who had never been sick a day in his life. It devastated him to be permanently incapacitated. One afternoon his daughter was attending to his needs and preparing his medication. As she leaned toward him to straighten his bed, she saw that he was crying. No one ever remembered seeing this proud, self-made man shed a tear. It shocked her and she said, "Daddy, what's wrong?"

He replied, "Honey, go get your mother."

My little grandmother came running up the stairs and knelt beside her husband's bed. He took her by the hand and said, "I know I'm going to die, and I'm not afraid of death. But it is so dark. Will you pray for me?"

My grandmother said, "Will I *pray?*" She had been waiting for him to ask her that question for more than 40 years! She began to call to heaven on behalf of her husband, and he accepted a personal relationship with Jesus Christ there on his sickbed. My grandmother said it was like a host of heavenly angels beginning to sing in her heart. Grandfather Dobson died two weeks later with a testimony on his lips. I'm certain that he and my little grandmother are in heaven today because of the perseverance of her faith.

Winston Churchill said during World War II, "Never give up. Never, never, never give up!" That advice applies not only to nations under siege but also to believers seeking a touch from the Almighty. I'll say it again: moms and dads, your highest priority is to lead your children into the fold. Don't stop praying until that objective is fulfilled.

Q3. **You wrote about human pride and the offense it is to God. I don't fully understand what that means. Shouldn't mankind be proud of our achievements and discoveries? Do you not admire the accomplishments of modern science, medicine, and the arts? What is wrong with a little self-satisfaction and confidence? Does God, if he exists, want us to grovel like beggars before Him?**

A3. As a former professor in a large university medical school, I have marveled at the miracles accomplished through research and scientific inquiry. I'm grateful we live in a day when vast knowledge is available to anyone who can get to a local library. These are remarkable times, to be sure, and we have reason to feel good about the effort to reduce human suffering and make a better life for us all. There is nothing offensive to God about progress per se.

But there is something inherently evil about the prevailing notion that man no longer needs God—that we can get along very well on our own, thank you. Even more odious is the New Age philosophy that grants godlike status to mere mortals. Its followers worship the human mind, as though that pound of wrinkled gray matter somehow produced itself from nothingness. The Shirley MacLaine clones proclaim with awe, "We only use 5 percent of our brains. Imagine what is possible if we would achieve our entire potential." I'm all for education, but this gee-whiz view of "human potential" is nonsense. If it were possible to employ 95 percent more brainpower, some bright soul among the 5 billion now living would have found a way to do it. And even if that happened, we would still have peanut-brains compared with the wisdom and omnipotence of the Almighty.

The word *arrogance* comes to mind in this context. Though we exist by the graciousness of a loving Lord, mankind is systematically seeking to overthrow Him as the moral authority of the universe. We've jettisoned His commandments and replaced them with our puny notions and ideas. Secular humanism has concluded that there are no eternal truths, no transcendent values, no ultimate rights and wrongs. What seems right at the time *is* right. Morality is determined by public opinion polls, as though our pooled ignorance will somehow produce verity. In the process, we have forgotten the faith of our fathers that was lovingly handed down to us and entrusted to our care.

Arrogance is not a new phenomenon in human society, of course. Jesus told us about a rich farmer who had no need for God. He had his life nicely laid out. He produced such a bumper crop that year that he couldn't even store it all. In a world of suffering and starvation, that was his biggest problem.

Then he said, "This is what I'll do. I will tear down my barns and build bigger ones, and there I will store all my grain and my goods. And I'll say to myself, 'You have plenty of good things laid up for many years. Take life easy; eat, drink and be merry.'"

But God said to him, "You fool! This very night your life will be demanded from you. Then who will get what you have prepared for yourself?" (Luke 12:18-20)

That rich farmer who basked in self-sufficiency is reminiscent of today's superstars and miracle men. Pick up any issue of *People* magazine and the aroma of human pride will waft from its pages. When I think of arrogance and contempt for God, for example, I am reminded of the deceased rock star, John Lennon. He and his fellow Beatles rebelled against everything holy and clean. They were involved in the most wicked homosexual and heterosexual orgies, and they popularized the use of marijuana and hard drugs among a generation of young people. We're still suffering from that plague. Some of their music, as melodic and clever as it was, reflected this decadence and set the stage for the demonic excesses of today's rock industry.

Lennon was also an outspoken atheist. One of his well-known compositions was a song entitled "Imagine," which postulated a world with no religion to wreak havoc on mankind. Lennon felt that patriotism and belief in God were responsible for war and other social ills. He said this in 1966:

> *Christianity will go. It will vanish and shrink. I needn't argue about that. I'm right and I will be proved right. We're more popular than Jesus now; I don't know which will go first—rock 'n' roll or Christianity. Jesus was all right, but his disciples were thick and ordinary. It's them twisting it that ruins it for me.* [2]

As it turned out, Lennon was the one to go, succumbing in 1980 to five bullets fired by a psychopath on the streets of New York City. The wages of John's sin turned out to be death. Now he must deal with the One who said, "Vengeance is mine; I will repay, saith the Lord" (Romans 12:19, KJV).

Any man is a fool, regardless of his intelligence or accomplishments, if he fails to reckon with the God of the universe. It's that simple.

Q4. **In trying to comprehend why God does what He does, I've wondered about the spirit world that is referred to in the Bible. Do you believe such an unseen realm really exists?**

A4. Yes, I do, although I do not profess to understand it. I know only that the Scripture speaks about a spiritual

2 *Time,* August 12, 1966, p. 38.

warfare that occurs in a dimension beyond human perception. It is not given to man to comprehend this struggle entirely at this period in our history. However, its existence and significance are unmistakable in Scripture.

We get a window into that unseen spirit world from Daniel as he saw it some 500 years before the birth of Christ. This intelligent young man was only 16 when Jerusalem was conquered by the Babylonians, and he was deported to Babylon along with his surviving countrymen. There he was elevated to political prominence and soon became God's prophetic voice to His people.

Some years later, Daniel had a terrifying vision in which he was visited by a heavenly messenger. Many Bible scholars believe that visitor was Christ Himself. Tucked within the first few verses of Daniel's narrative is a fascinating glimpse of the spirit world we cannot see and the conflict between good and evil that occurs there:

I looked up and there before me was a man dressed in linen, with a belt of the finest gold around his waist. His body was like chrysolite, his face like lightning, his eyes like flaming torches, his arms and legs like the gleam of burnished bronze, and his voice like the sound of a multitude.

I, Daniel, was the only one who saw the vision; the men with me did not see it, but such terror overwhelmed them that they fled and hid themselves. So I was left alone, gazing at this great vision; I had no strength left, my face turned deathly pale and I was helpless. Then I heard him speaking, and as I listened to him, I fell into a deep sleep, my face to the ground.

A hand touched me and set me trembling on my hands and knees. He said, "Daniel, you who are highly esteemed, consider carefully the words I am about to speak to you, and stand up, for I have now been sent to you." And when he said this to me, I stood up trembling.

Then he continued, "Do not be afraid, Daniel. Since the first day that you set your mind to gain understanding and to humble yourself before your God, your words were heard, and I have come in response to them. But the prince of the Persian kingdom resisted me twenty-one days. Then Michael, one of the chief princes, came to help me, because I was detained there with the king of Persia." (Daniel 10:5-13)

There are several fascinating and tantalizing elements to this account. First, it is surprising that a man of Daniel's stature (being "highly esteemed" in God's eyes) did not receive an instantaneous answer to his prayer. He had to wait three weeks before the reply from the Lord came back. What is more interesting is the reason for the delay. Although Daniel's prayer was answered immediately, it took 21 days for the "messenger" to fight his way past the satanic beings who stood in his way. If the visitor was, in fact, Jesus Christ, what does that say about the power temporarily held by the forces of evil?

Finally, I wish we understood more about the celestial warfare hinted at by the messenger. Later in the conversation with Daniel, he said, "Soon I will return to fight against the prince of Persia, and when I go, the prince of Greece will come" (v. 20). The implications of this passage are striking. We get the picture of the entire earth being divided into territories and jurisdictions led by powerful beings whose mission it is to oppose the will of God. Perhaps a high-ranking demon is assigned to each church and every Christian college, as Frank Peretti suggested in *This Present Darkness*.

If this sounds farfetched, consider Paul's warning about our enemy. He wrote, "For our struggle is not against flesh and blood, but against the rulers, against the authorities, against the powers of this dark world and against the spiritual forces of evil in the heavenly realms" (Ephesians 6:12).

How can we prevail spiritually against so dangerous and powerful an enemy? We can't in our own strength, but thank the Lord, He can. The Scripture assures us that "the one who is in you is greater than the one who is in the world" (1 John 4:4). Furthermore, there are reassuring words found in other relevant Scriptures. Let's examine one of the most encouraging.

We spoke earlier of Elijah, who was sent by God to hide by the brook Kerith. Look now at Elijah's successor, Elisha, as recorded in 2 Kings 6. The evil king of Syria hated Elisha and heard he was living in Dothan.

One night, he sent a great army with many horses and chariots to capture the prophet. These soldiers camped around the city until dawn, knowing that they had their enemy trapped. The next morning, Elisha's servant arose early and discovered the forces arrayed against them. He ran back to the prophet and said anxiously, "Oh, my lord, what shall we do?" (v. 15).

The great man of God said, "Don't be afraid, . . . those who are with us are more than those who are with them" (v. 16).

His servant must have been mystified. Only the two of them were standing there. Then Elisha asked the Lord to open the eyes of the young man, and suddenly he saw horses and chariots of fire all over the surrounding mountains. There was an entire army of heavenly beings waiting to fight the battle for the Lord.

How exciting to know that there are unseen warriors around us in times of satanic attack. Is that still true today? Well, we're told in Psalm 34:7, "The angel of the Lord encamps around those who fear him, and he delivers them." Psalm 91:11 says, "For he will command his angels concerning you to guard you in all your ways." Hebrews 12:1 tells us that we are surrounded by a "great cloud of witnesses." It is indeed, comforting to know that we are not alone, even in the midst of a spiritual battle. Furthermore, it should be remembered that all the angels, including those who minister to our needs, were involved in a heavenly war before the dawn of creation. We're not given the details of that conflict, but we do understand that Satan and his demons were defeated by God and His angels. Therefore, it is reasonable to assume that the angelic beings who "encamp around" us are experienced in dealing with the forces of evil. And if they need help, they can appeal to the One about whom it is written, "If God is for us, who can be against us?" (Romans 8:31).

Q5. **How do you think this unseen spiritual world influences our day-by-day activities in this Christian walk?**

A5. I don't know, but it makes for interesting speculation. Let me share a personal experience just to contemplate the possibilities. Some years ago, I was engaged in research that required me to visit 16 major medical centers each year. One of those trips took me to New York City where I fulfilled my hospital responsibilities and then took a few hours off for sight-seeing. Two colleagues joined me on a makeshift tour of the Big Apple. It was a pleasant day, and we chatted amiably as we moved around the city on the subway system.

Suddenly, one of my associates said, "Hey! Take a look at that weird guy standing over there on the platform. Wasn't he with us on the last two trains?"

We each remembered that the man had definitely been near us for at least one-half hour. Now he stood watching us intently from about 30 feet away. Before we could figure out what he was up to, we realized our next train had pulled into the station. We scurried aboard at the last second and the doors closed behind us. The grubby guy ran toward us but didn't make it. He became furious when he couldn't get the automatic doors to open. He jumped on the side of the train, screaming obscenities and threats at us. Then he had to let go as our speed accumulated. The last I saw of him, he was waving his arms and shouting invectives as we rode out of the station.

My friends and I discussed the shocking behavior and wondered about the man's intentions. What had he planned to do? Had we been spared an act of violence by boarding the train? Who knows? The only thing certain is that we were marked by this man for some kind of surprise—probably an unpleasant one. Perhaps we avoided a life-threatening experience by what seemed like sheer coincidence.

It is possible, of course, that the Lord specifically intervened to protect us in the subway. We were totally off guard and vulnerable to the secret plans of this possible psychopath or drug addict or killer. Just contemplating what might have been raised the broader question of how frequently in our lifetimes we might have been spared dangerous consequences that we never recognized. It is an interesting thought. Who can know how often the Lord quietly protects us, redirects us, or leads us on safer paths?

There are other occasions when we almost seem preordained for tragedy. I remember seeing a terrible collision on a Los Angeles freeway as I was coming home from work one afternoon. The first car crashed through the center divider and struck an oncoming Pontiac head-on. Both drivers were killed instantly. I have thought often about the incredible timing that was necessary to produce that wreck. If the two men were each going 60 miles per hour, they were approaching one another at a combined speed of 120 miles per hour. Computed another way, their cars were coming together at the rate of 176 feet per second. If the man in the first car had been early by one-tenth of a second, the driver of the second car would probably have been past the original point of collision by the time of the accident. The car behind the second driver might have been the one to be struck. When you think about it, the most infinitesimal change in either man's day would have saved the second man's life. Most fatal accidents, in this way, depend on split-second timing if they are to occur as they do.

Our lives literally hang by a thread even when we are oblivious to a particular danger. Does it not seem wise, given what is at stake, for us to bathe every day and each activity in prayer? James addressed this tentative grip on life, saying,

> Now listen, you who say, "Today or tomorrow we will go to this or that city, spend a year there, carry on business and make money." Why, you do not even know what will happen tomorrow. What is your life? You are a mist that appears for a little while and then vanishes. Instead, you ought to say,

"If it is the Lord's will, we will live and do this or that." (James 4:13-15)

The bottom line is that our welfare on this mortal coil is influenced by forces that are beyond the scope of our intellect. We are caught up in a struggle between good and evil that plays a significant, although unidentified, role in our lives. Our task, then, is not to decipher exactly how these pieces fit and what it all means, but to remain faithful and obedient to Him who knows all mysteries.

11

BEYOND THE BETRAYAL BARRIER

We come now to our final comments regarding this vitally important topic: when God doesn't make sense. Our message boils down to this very simple understanding: there is nothing the Lord wants of us more than the exercise of our faith. He will do nothing to undermine it, and we cannot please him without it. To define the term again, *faith* is believing that which has no absolute proof (Hebrews 11:1). It is hanging tough when the evidence would have us bail out. It is determining to trust him when he has not answered all the questions or even assured a pain-free passage.

There is no better illustration of this faithfulness than is seen in the second half of Hebrews chapter 11. This Scripture, to which we referred earlier, has been called the "heroes' hall of fame," and it bears great relevance to our discussion. Described therein are the men and women who persevered in their faith under the most extreme circumstances. They were subjected to every kind of hardship and danger for the sake of the Cross. Some were tortured, imprisoned, flogged, stoned, sawed in two, and put to death by the sword. They were destitute, mistreated, persecuted, and inadequately clothed. They wandered in the deserts, in mountains, in caves, and in holes in the ground. Most important for our topic, they died not receiving what had been promised. In other words, they held onto their faith to the point of death, even though God had not explained what he was doing (Hebrews 11:35-40).

Without detracting from the sacredness of that Scripture, I would like to submit for your inspiration my own modern day "heroes' hall of fame." Listed among these giants of the faith are some incredible human beings who must hold a special place in the great heart of God.

At the top of my list would have to be some of the boys and girls I knew during my 14 years on the Attending Staff at Children's Hospital, Los Angeles. Most of these kids suffered from terminal illnesses, although others endured chronic disorders that disrupted and warped their childhoods. Some of them were under 10 years of age, and yet their faith in Jesus Christ was unshakable. They died with a testimony on their lips, witnessing to the goodness of God while their little bodies withered away. What a reception they must have received when they met him who said, "Suffer the little children to come unto me" (Mark 10:14, KJV).

In my first film series, Focus on the Family, I shared a story about a five-year-old African-American boy who will never be forgotten by those who knew him. A nurse with whom I worked, Gracie Schaeffler, had taken care of this lad during the latter days of his life. He was dying of lung cancer, which is a terrifying disease in its final stages. The lungs fill with fluid, and the patient is unable to breathe. It is terribly claustrophobic, especially for a small child.

This little boy had a Christian mother who loved him and stayed by his side through the long ordeal. She cradled him on her lap and talked softly about the Lord. Instinctively, the woman was preparing her son for the final hours to come. Gracie told me that she entered his room one day as death approached, and she heard this lad talking about hearing bells ring.

"The bells are ringing, Mommie," he said. "I can hear them."

Gracie thought he was hallucinating because he was already slipping away. She left and returned a few minutes later and again heard him talking about hearing bells ring.

The nurse said to his mother, "I'm sure you know your baby is hearing things that aren't there. He is hallucinating because of the sickness."

The mother pulled her son closer to her chest, smiled, and said, "No, Miss Schaeffler. He is not hallucinating. I told him when he was frightened—when he couldn't breathe—if he would listen carefully, he could hear the bells of heaven ringing for him. That is what he's been talking about all day."

That precious child died on his mother's lap later that evening, and he was still talking about the bells of heaven when the angels came to take him. What a brave little trooper he was. His courage was not reported in the newspapers the next day. Neither Tom Brokaw nor Dan Rather told his story on the evening news. Yet he and his mother belong forever in our "heroes' hall of fame."

My next candidate for faithful immortality is a man I never met, although he touched my life while he was losing his. I learned about him from a docudrama on television that I saw many years ago. The producer had obtained permission from a cancer specialist to place cameras in his clinic. Then with approval from three patients, two men and a woman, he captured on film the moment each of them learned they were afflicted with a malignancy in its later stages. Their initial shock, disbelief, fear, and anger were recorded in graphic detail. Afterwards, the documentary team followed these three families through the treatment process with its ups and downs, hopes and disappointments, pain and terror. I sat riveted as the drama of life and death unfolded on the screen. Eventually, all three patients died, and the program ended without comment or editorial.

There was so much that should have been said. What struck me were the different ways these people dealt with their frightening circumstances. The two who apparently had no faith reacted with anger and bitterness. They not only fought their disease, but they seemed to be at war with everyone else. Their personal relationships and even their marriages were shaken, especially as the end drew near. I'm not being critical, mind you. Most of us would respond in much the same manner if faced with imminent death. But that's what made the third individual so inspiring to me.

He was a humble black pastor of a small inner-city Baptist church. He was in his late sixties and had been a minister throughout his adult life. His love for the Lord was so profound that it was reflected in everything he said. When he and his wife were told he had only a few months to live, they revealed no panic. They quietly asked the doctor what it all meant. When he had explained the treatment program and what they could anticipate, they politely thanked him for his concern and departed. The cameras followed this little couple to their old car and eavesdropped as they bowed their heads and recommitted themselves to the Lord.

In the months that followed, the pastor never lost his poise. Nor was he glib about his illness. He was not in denial. He simply had come to terms with the cancer and its probable outcome. He knew the Lord was in control, and he refused to be shaken in his faith.

The cameras were present on his final Sunday in his church. He actually preached the sermon that morning and talked openly about his impending death. To the best of my recollection, this is what he said:

"Some of you have asked me if I'm mad at God for this disease that has taken over my body. I'll tell you honestly that I have nothing but love in my heart for my Lord. He didn't do this to me. We live in a sinful world where sickness and death are the curse man has brought on himself. And I'm going to a better place where there will be no more tears, no suffering, and no heartache. So don't feel bad for me.

"Besides," he continued, "our Lord suffered and died for our sins. Why should I not share in his suffering?" Then he began to sing, without accompaniment, in an old, broken voice:

Must Jesus bear the cross alone,
And all the world go free?
No, there's a cross for everyone,
And there's a cross for me.

How happy are the saints above,
Who once went sorr'wing here;
But now they taste unmingled love,
And joy without a tear.

The consecrated cross I'll bear,
Till death shall set me free,
And then go home my crown to wear,
For there's a crown for me.

I wept as this gentle man sang of his love for Jesus. He sounded very weak, and his face was drawn from the ravages of the disease. But his comments were as powerful as any I've ever heard. His words that morning were his last from the pulpit, as far as I know. He slipped into eternity a few days later, where he met the Lord he had served for a lifetime. This unnamed pastor and his wife have a prominent place among my spiritual heroes.

I will tell you about one more inductee into my hall of fame. She is a woman named Marian Benedict Manwell, who is still living. I was first introduced to her in a letter she wrote to me in 1979, and I never forgot what she said. I have kept that letter all these years, and in fact, I called her this week. I found this delightful lady still holding tightly to her faith in Jesus Christ. But let me share what she wrote me in that original correspondence so many years ago.

Dear Dr. Dobson:

I'm going to tell you my experience as an "ugly duckling." I was the first child of a young minister and his school-marm wife. They were about 30 years old when I was born. (Now brace yourself for this.) When I was 8 months of age, the heavy spring of the jumper in which I was bouncing suddenly snapped. Being taut, it came straight down and tore through the first thing it hit—the soft spot on my head.

There was nothing to be done. My parents and my uncle and aunt (with whom we were vacationing) believed me to be dead. They finally found a doctor who took me to the hospital eight miles away, but there was nothing they could do but cleanse and bandage the wound. They gave my parents no hope at all that I would live.

They were godly people and they believed in prayer, as did all our relatives and friends. Their faith is responsible for my life. By the mercy of God I lived, even though the doctors told my family I would be a hopeless cripple and mentally incompetent. That did not happen, but there were many problems.

To begin with, I was not a beautiful child. I was very homely, and gimpy too. Oh yes, I walked. The

Lord saw to that when he healed me of total paralysis. I was also blessed with a quick mind. Still, as you have written, people look for beauty in children. My younger brother had the beauty of the family. He looked like our dad, auburn hair, brown eyes, and he was a charmer. I could not run, or jump rope, or play ball, or catch anything thrown to me. I was crippled on my left side. I guess that's why I became a loner. I developed an imagination that allowed me to live a wonderful life through the hundreds of books that I read and the daydreams I invented.

When I told my mother, who died of cancer when I was 10 years old, that I wanted to be a nurse and a missionary, she said, "That's wonderful." She knew that I could never be either because of my infirmity. Then we moved to another small town when our father remarried two years after my mother's death. Things became even more difficult. I was not popular through high school. I was a P.K., a preacher's kid. And long before this time I had given my heart to the Lord. That, added to my introverted personality, did not draw me into the cliques of our little town school.

One day as I trudged along the walk to the school, a teenage boy came up behind me and asked loudly, "What's wrong with you? What's ya limping for? Nobody wants to go with a girl that acts like that."

I had a very difficult time learning that Christ

*could give me the strength to be calm and composed
in such a situation.*

Let me interrupt Mrs. Manwell's letter briefly to
summarize the circumstances she shared. This child
was neurologically handicapped from infancy and unable to play like other boys and girls. The rejection of
her peers forced her to meet her social needs through
her fantasies. She almost casually mentioned the death
of a very sensitive and caring mother when she was 10,
and the arrival of a stepmother at the beginning of
adolescence. Add to that the ridicule of the opposite
sex as a teenager and further rejection because she was
a preacher's kid. Here are the ingredients for lifelong
psychological damage in most children. But this was no
ordinary young lady.

Let's return to the letter to see what the Lord has
done with her life:

*Later, I married a boy I went to school with, and the
Lord has blessed me with six sons and two daughters! All of them are married to wonderful Christian
mates. For almost 40 years now, Clinton has protected me, sometimes when I would foolishly have
bitten off more than I could chew. He has given me
the confidence I needed to use the imagination that
I developed as a child (to write poetry and short
stories).*

*It is so rewarding to see our children leading lives
as respected and honored members of their com-*

munities and as caring members of their mate's families. My older daughter came home from a visit with a former school friend two or three years ago and was shocked to learn that many of her former classmates were dropouts from life—they were on drugs or were drinking heavily. They were divorced or were unwed parents. Some were in prison.

Beth said, "When I see our big family that often did not have any of the nice things of life and yet everyone is a solid, law-abiding citizen, I have so much to be thankful for. I think you must have prayed a lot for us."

And I cried. That's the most rewarding aspect of parenthood for me. Thank you for letting me use so much of your time, Dr. Dobson, and God bless you.

Marian Benedict Manwell

Thank you, Marian, for revealing your faithfulness to us. You could easily have blamed God for making life so difficult. Even as a child, I'm sure you understood that He could have prevented that spring from breaking, or redirected it away from your head. He didn't have to take your mother when you needed her so badly. He could have made you pretty, or popular, or athletic. It would have been reasonable, given these limitations, for you to have been bitter at the Lord. The deck did seem stacked against you. But nowhere in your letter was there a hint of anger or disillusionment. Nor do we sense any self-pity as you described your plight. Instead, as you told us, "Long before this time, I had given my heart to the Lord."

I admire you greatly, Marian Benedict Manwell. The Lord must feel the same. Although He seemed not to care in those early days, He was quietly working behind the scenes to send a Christian husband to love and protect you. Then He blessed you with eight children, each of them growing up to serve Him. What a capstone to a life of faith! If you had yielded to bitterness because of your handicap, your sons and daughters would certainly have observed it. Some probably would have adopted the same attitude. Thank you for holding tightly to your faith even when God made no sense in the affairs of your life! You are also a cherished member of my all-time hall of fame.

There are more heroes in my catalog than I could describe in many volumes this size, but I will resist the inclination to name them. Our purpose, as you know, has been to help those who are not so well grounded in their beliefs. If everyone was gifted with the tenacity of a bulldog and the faith of Father Abraham, there would be no need for a discussion of this nature. But most of us are not spiritual superstars. That's why these thoughts have been dedicated affectionately to individuals who have been wounded in spirit by experiences they could not understand. The pieces to life's puzzle simply have not fit together, leaving them confused, angry, and disillusioned.

Perhaps you are among those who have struggled to comprehend a particular heartache and God's reason for allowing it. A thousand unanswered questions have been recycling in your mind—most of them beginning with *"Why . . . ?"* You want desperately to trust the Father and believe in His grace and goodness. But deep inside, you're held captive by a sense of betrayal and abandonment. The Lord obviously permitted your difficulties to occur. Why didn't He prevent them—and why has He not attempted to explain or apologize for them? The inability to answer those fundamental questions has become a spiritual barrier a mile high, and you can't seem to find a way around or over it.

For some of you, your sorrow can be traced directly to the death of a precious son or daughter. Your pain from that loss has been so intense that you've wondered if you could even carry on. What a joy he (or she) was to your heart. He ran and jumped and giggled and hugged. You loved him far more than you valued your own life. But then, there was that horrible morning at the pool, or the ominous medical report, or the accident on the bicycle. Now your beloved child is gone, and God's purpose in his death has remained a mystery.

For someone else, there will never be anything as painful as the rejection you were dealt by an ex-husband or wife. The day you discovered the infidelity, or when the divorce papers arrived at the door, or that unforgettable night of violence—those were indescribable moments of heartache. In some ways, it would have been easier to have buried the spouse than to see him or her in the arms of another. How could that person to whom you gave everything be so cruel? Many tears were shed as God was begged to intervene. When the marriage continued to fail, disillusionment and bitterness rolled over you like a tidal wave. You've said you would never trust anyone again—not even the Almighty.

I'm thinking also of the widows and widowers who are trying to survive on their own. If you are one of them, you know that very few of your friends fully comprehend. They want you to get over this loss and return to the business of living. But you just can't do it. For so many years, your marriage was the centerpiece of your existence. Two separate human beings truly became "one flesh" as God intended. It was such a sweet love affair that could have gone on forever. In fact, when you were young you honestly thought it would. But suddenly, it was over. And now for the first time in many years, you are truly alone. Is this what it all comes down to?

My mother never did recover from the death of my dad. He left her suddenly at the family table one Sunday afternoon at 66 years of age. Though she lived 11 years beyond that day, her heart was broken and it never healed. She had built her life around the man who swept her off her feet in 1934, and she simply could not face the future without him. My mother didn't blame God for his passing, but she suffered nonetheless. This is what she wrote in her diary near the first anniversary of my father's death:

People have told me that the first year was the hardest. It's been one year and three days since you died, and tonight I am frantic with longing for you. Oh dear God! It's more than I can bear. The sobs make my heart skip beats. I cannot see the paper. My head throbs. The house is lonely and still. Visions of you have been as real as if you were here and had not left me. Today I thanked God for letting an angel watch over me. But how desperately I missed you!

It is very cold outside. Last night, a sleet storm covered the earth with ice and then froze into a solid crust. The streets are slippery and dangerous. I hate it. It makes me feel blue, frightened, and alone. I dread the winter to follow. It will last for three more months.

I moved into the smaller bedroom today. I wish you were here to share that room with me. There are precious memories there. When I was ill four years ago, you prayed for me in that bedroom during the midnight hours. You lay on the floor, agonizing in prayer for me. We both knew the Spirit was praying through you. Later the Lord led us to a doctor who helped me find my way back to health. Oh how I loved you. I love your memory today.

What a special lady my mother was, and how profoundly she loved my father! She is with him in heaven now. But there are other widows and widowers out there who loved just as deeply and now must face the future alone. I extend to each of them my love and prayers as they take one day at a time.

There are so many other sources of pain. I am mindful of those among my readers who are hurting for less catastrophic reasons, such as adult children of alcoholics, those who have been overweight from childhood, those who were physically or sexually abused in the early years, and people who are blind, quadriplegic, chronically ill, etc. I'm also concerned for the single mothers who wonder how long they can carry the load that is on their shoulders. A million different scenarios exist, but they all point to a similar kind of frustration. And most of them bear theological implications.

To those whom I have been describing—those who have struggled to understand God's providence—I bring hope to you today! No, I can't provide tidy little solutions to all of life's annoying inconsistencies. That will not occur until we see the Lord face-to-face. But his heart is especially tender toward the downtrodden and the defeated. He knows your name and he has seen every tear you have shed. He was there on each occasion when life took a wrong turn. And what appears to be divine disinterest or cruelty is a misunderstanding at best and a satanic lie at worst.

How do I know this to be true? Because the Scriptures emphatically tell us so. For starters, David wrote, "The Lord is close to the brokenhearted and saves those who are crushed in spirit" (Psalm 34:18). Isn't that a beautiful verse? How encouraging to know that the very presence of the King—the Creator of all heaven and earth—hovers near to those who are wounded and discouraged. If you could fully comprehend how deeply you are loved, you would never feel alone again. David returned to that thought in Psalm 103:11: "For as high as the heavens are above the earth, so great is his love for those who fear him."

Another favorite passage of mine is Romans 8:26, in which we're told that the Holy Spirit actually prays for you and me with such passion that human language is inadequate to describe it. That verse says, "In the same way, the Spirit helps us in our weakness. We do not know what we ought to pray for, but the Spirit himself intercedes for us with groans that words cannot express." What comfort we should draw from that understanding! He is calling your name to the Father today, pleading your case and describing your need. How wrong it is, therefore, to place the blame for your troubles on the best Friend mankind ever had! Regardless of other conclusions you draw, please believe this: He is not the source of your pain!

If you were sitting before me at this moment, you might be inclined to ask, "Then how do you explain the tragedies and hardships that have come into my life? Why did God do this to me?" My reply, which you've read in previous pages, is not profound. But I know it is right! God usually does not choose to answer those questions in this life! That's what I've been trying to say. He will not parade His plans and purposes for our approval. We must never forget that He is God. As such

He wants us to believe and trust in him despite the things we don't understand. It's that straightforward.

Jehovah never did answer Job's intelligent inquiries, and He will not respond to all of yours. Every person who ever lived, I submit, has had to deal with seeming contradictions and enigmas. You will not be the exception. If that explanation is unsatisfactory and you can't accept it, then you are destined to go through life with a weak, ineffectual faith—or no faith at all. You'll just have to construct your castles on some other foundation. That will be your greatest challenge, however— because there is no other foundation. It is written, "Unless the Lord builds the house, its builders labor in vain" (Psalm 127:1).

My strongest advice is that each of us acknowledge *before* the crisis occurs, if possible, that our trust in Him must be independent of our understanding. There's nothing wrong with trying to understand, but we must not lean on our ability to comprehend! Sooner or later our intellect will pose questions we cannot possibly answer. At that point, we would be wise to remember His words, "As the heavens are higher than the earth, so are my ways higher than your ways and my thoughts than your thoughts" (Isaiah 55:9). And our reply should be, "Not my will, but yours be done" (Luke 22:42).

When you think about it, there is comfort in that approach to life's trials and tribulations. We are relieved from the responsibility of trying to figure them out. We haven't been given enough information to decipher the code. It is enough to acknowledge that God makes sense even when He doesn't make sense. Does this approach seem a bit simplistic, like an explanation we would give a child? Yes, and for good reason. Jesus put it like this, "I tell you the truth, anyone who will not receive the kingdom of God like a little child will never enter it" (Luke 18:17).

But what do we say to the person who just can't grasp that truth? What advice is available for that individual who is bitter and deeply angry at God for some perceived misdeed? How can he or she circumvent the betrayal barrier and begin a new relationship with the Lord?

There is only one cure for the cancer of bitterness. That is to forgive the perceived offender once and for all, with God's help. As strange as it seems, I am suggesting that some of us need to forgive God for those heartaches that are charged to His account. You've carried resentment against Him for years. Now it's time to let go of it. Please don't misunderstand me at this point. God is in the business of forgiving us, and it almost sounds blasphemous to suggest that the relationship could be reversed. He has done no wrong and does not need our approbation. But the source of bitterness must be admitted before it can be cleansed. There is no better way to get rid of it than to absolve the Lord of whatever we have harbored, and then ask His forgiveness for our lack of faith. It's called reconciliation, and it is the only way you will ever be entirely free.

The late Corrie ten Boom would have understood the advice I've given today. She and her family were sent by the Nazis to an extermination camp at Ravensbruck,

Germany, during the latter years of World War II. They suffered horrible cruelty and deprivation at the hands of S.S. guards and, ultimately, only Corrie survived. After the war, she became a celebrated author and spoke often on the love of God and His intervention in her life. But inside, she was still bitter at the Nazis for what they had done to herself and her family.

Two years after the war, Corrie was speaking in Munich, Germany, on the subject of God's forgiveness. After the service, she saw a man making his way toward her. This is what she would later write about that encounter:

> *And that's when I saw him, working his way forward against the others. One moment I saw the overcoat and the brown hat; the next, a blue uniform and a visored cap with its skull and crossbones. It came back with a rush: the huge room with its harsh overhead lights; the pathetic pile of dresses and shoes in the center of the floor; the shame of walking naked past this man. I could see my sister's frail form ahead of me, ribs sharp beneath the parchment skin. Betsie, how thin you were!*
>
> *The place was Ravensbruck and the man who was making his way forward had been a guard— one of the most cruel guards.*
>
> *Now he was in front of me, hand thrust out.*
>
> *"A fine message, Fraülein! How good it is to know that, as you say, all our sins are at the bottom of the sea!"*

And I, who had spoken so glibly of forgiveness, fumbled in my pocketbook rather than take that hand. He would not remember me, of course—how could he remember one prisoner among those thousands of women?

But I remembered him and the leather crop swinging from his belt. I was face-to-face with one of my captors and my blood seemed to freeze.

"You mentioned Ravensbruck in your talk," he was saying. "I was a guard there." No, he did not remember me.

"But since that time," he went on, "I have become a Christian. I know that God has forgiven me for the cruel things I did there, but I would like to hear from your lips as well. Fraulein,"—again the hand came out—"will you forgive me?"

And I stood there—I whose sins had again and again to be forgiven—and could not forgive. Betsie had died in that place—could he erase her slow terrible death simply for the asking?

It could not have been many seconds that he stood there—hand held out—but to me it seemed hours as I wrestled with the most difficult thing I had ever had to do.

For I had to do it—I knew that. The message that God forgives has a prior condition: that we forgive those who have injured us. "If you do not forgive men their trespasses," Jesus says, "neither will your Father in heaven forgive your trespasses."

I knew it not only as a commandment of God, but

as a daily experience. Since the end of the war I had had a home in Holland for victims of Nazi brutality. Those who were able to forgive their former enemies were able also to return to the outside world and rebuild their lives, no matter what the physical scars. Those who nursed their bitterness remained invalids. It was as simple and horrible as that.

And still I stood there with the coldness clutching my heart. But forgiveness is not an emotion—I knew that too. Forgiveness is an act of the will, and the will can function regardless of the temperatures of the heart. "Jesus, help me!" I prayed silently. "I can lift my hand. I can do that much. You supply the feeling."

And so woodenly, mechanically, I thrust my hand into the one stretched out to me. And as I did, an incredible thing took place. The current started in my shoulder, raced down my arm, sprang into our joined hands. And then this healing warmth seemed to flood my whole being, bringing tears to my eyes.

"I forgive you, brother," I cried. "With all my heart."

For a long moment we grasped each other's hands, the former guard and the former prisoner. I had never known God's love so intensely, as I did then. But even so, I realized it was not my love. I had tried, and did not have the power. It was the power of the Holy Spirit as recorded in Romans 5:5,

". . . because the love of God is shed abroad in our hearts by the Holy Ghost which is given unto us."[1]

Corrie's words have great relevance for us at this point. Bitterness of all varieties, including that which is seemingly "justified," will destroy a person spiritually and emotionally. It is a sickness of the soul. Corrie forgave an S.S. guard who shared responsibility for the deaths of her family members; surely, we can forgive the King of the universe who sent his only Son to die as an atonement for our sins.

Before we close, there is a particular person whom I want to address directly. I am especially concerned about that individual among my readers who is facing a terminal illness at this time. You've learned more than you ever wanted to know about chemotherapy, radiation, MRI's, liver biopsies, angioplasties, CAT scans, or abdominal surgery. Any one of these procedures (and a thousand others) is enough to demoralize the most secure among us. Perhaps you are not angry at God in the way I have described, but you are hurt, confused, and demoralized. You've wondered, with proper respect, why God would let this happen to you. I believe I have a word from the Lord that may be helpful to you. I certainly hope so.

It is so important to understand that God's value system is entirely different from our own—and His is correct. In human eyes, death is viewed as the ultimate

1 Corrie ten Boom, *Tramp for the Lord* (Old Tappan, N.J.: Revell, 1976), pp. 53-55.

defeat—the final tragedy. As such, it hangs over our heads from early childhood like the sword of Damocles.

My first encounter with death occurred when I was barely three years of age. I had become friends with a two-year-old whose parents were members of the church my father pastored. His name was Danny, and he came to visit me one day. We dressed up like cowboys and walked around shooting at things with toy guns. I remember trying to teach the little fellow how the game was played.

A few days later, Danny contracted an infection of some type and died very quickly. I didn't understand what had happened to him, although I knew my parents were upset. They took me with them to the funeral home but left me in the car for what seemed like an hour or more. Finally, my father came to get me. I was taken inside and shown the casket of my little friend. Dad then held me up so I could see Danny's body. I remember believing he was asleep, and that I could have awakened him if they would let me open his eyes. After we got back in the car, my parents tried to explain what had happened to Danny.

That was my first awareness that bad things can happen to good people. A short time later the same thing happened to my grandmother, and I began to get the picture. That gradual awareness of death is rather typical for preschool kids. Their dogs and cats die, and then they lose a grandparent or another member of the family. Some children, especially those in the inner city, learn about dying from the violence they witness in the streets.

Regardless of how it comes to be understood, death has a profound impact on our outlook and behavior from that point forward. For most of us, it represents the ultimate tragedy—the end to everything familiar and predictable. It bears the aura of the unknown—as depicted in horror movies and "scenes from beyond the grave." It is usually associated with disease, accidents, and violence, all having threatening overtones for us all.

Given this lifelong orientation, a diagnosis of a terminal illness (or the loss of a loved one) bears awesome implications for us psychologically and spiritually. I'm sure it will always be that way, and these words will not change it. But we need to understand that God views death very differently than we. It is no disaster to him. Isaiah 57:1 states, "The righteous perish, and no one ponders it in his heart; devout men are taken away, and no one understands that the righteous are taken away to be spared from evil." In other words, the righteous are far better off in the next world than in this one. Psalm 116:15 puts it more succinctly: "Precious in the sight of the Lord is the death of his saints."

What do these Scriptures mean for the living? They hint at a place on the far side of the river that is more wonderful than we can imagine. That is, in fact, precisely what we read in 1 Corinthians 2:9: "No eye has seen, no ear has heard, no mind has conceived what

God has prepared for those who love him." How reassuring it is to know that our loved ones have gone on to that better world and that we as believers will soon join them!

Does this sound like "pie in the sky by and by"—or perhaps "the opiate of the people," as Karl Marx sarcastically described it? Sure it does, but the Bible teaches it and I believe it. And because I do, death has taken on an entirely new dimension for me.

In a recent telephone conversation with the Rev. Billy Graham, whom I admire tremendously for his consistent walk with the Lord, I mentioned his ongoing battle with Parkinson's disease. Having watched that illness ravage the mind and body of my mother, I asked him, "Does your faith hold you steady at this stage of your life? Do you still believe what you did when you were young?"

The godly evangelist immediately replied with great emotion, "Oh, Jim, I can hardly wait to see my Lord!"

That is the biblical response to death. It is not a tragedy—it is a triumph! We should see it as a transition to the unfathomable joys and fellowship of eternal life. I heard a man who understood this concept beautifully. His last words before dying were, "This should be interesting."

Paul put it like this: "O death, where is thy sting? O grave, where is thy victory?" (1 Corinthians 15:55, KJV). Then toward the end of life he said, "For to me, to live is Christ and to die is gain" (Philippians 1:21).

If you have recently lost a child or a loved one, or

are facing death yourself, I don't want to minimize your pain. But I hope you will see that the discomfort is intensified by a misunderstanding of *time*. Our journey here has the illusion of permanence about it. Billions who went before us thought the same thing. Now they are gone—every one of them. In truth, we're just passing through. If we fully comprehended the brevity of life, the things that frustrate us—including most of those occasions when God doesn't make sense— wouldn't matter so much.

This is a vitally important biblical concept. David wrote, "As for man, his days are like grass, he flourishes like a flower of the field; the wind blows over it and it is gone, and its place remembers it no more" (Psalm 103:15-16). He also said, "Show me, O Lord, my life's end and the number of my days; let me know how fleeting is my life" (Psalm 39:4). Moses expressed the same idea in Psalm 90:12, "Teach us to number our days aright, that we may gain a heart of wisdom." That "wisdom" of which Moses spoke puts everything into proper perspective. It is difficult to get excited over raw materialism, for example, when one remembers that everything in this life is temporary.

That thought occurred to me one day when I was taking a commercial airline flight. We taxied out to the end of the runway and waited for clearance to take off. I looked out the window and saw the remains of two huge 747 airplanes sitting on the field. All the paint had been stripped off the fuselage and rust was spreading down from the top. The insides had been gutted and the windows were sealed. Then I saw a tiny bit of blue paint on the tail of one plane and realized these had been proud ships in the fleet of Pan American Airways.

The empty hulks looked pitiful sitting out there alone, shorn of their beauty. For some reason, they reminded me of the poem entitled "Little Boy Blue" by Eugene Field (1850–1895). The first stanza reads:

The little toy dog is covered with dust,
But sturdy and staunch he stands
And the little toy soldier is red with rust,
And his musket molds in his hands.
Time was when the little toy dog was new,
And the soldier was passing fair;
And that was the time when our Little Boy Blue
Kissed them and put them there.

I might have composed my own poem as I sat looking out the window:

Time was when these two airplanes were new
And they flew to great heights in the sky.
But now they are rusty, forgotten, and old
And they seem to be questioning, "Why?"

I imagined the day these magnificent craft were rolled out of the Boeing plant with shiny new enamel and the proud Pan Am insignia on their tails. They were christened with champagne amidst cheers and laughter. Then they were taken on their maiden voyages. Little boys and girls craned their necks skyward to watch these beautiful birds come in for a landing. What excitement they must have generated for passengers and crew.

Now, the company that owned them has gone bankrupt, and the planes are grounded forever. How could it happen in fewer than 20 years? Who would have thought these multimillion-dollar aircraft would come to such a quick and ignoble end?

As we taxied past the shells, I thought about the impermanence of everything that now looks so stable. Nothing lasts very long. And we are the ones who are passing through, on our way to another life of far greater significance.

To those who are hurting and discouraged at this time, I think it would be comforting to look forward to the time when the present trials will be a distant memory. A day of celebration is coming like nothing that has ever occurred in the history of mankind. The guest of honor on that morning will be one wearing a seamless robe, with eyes like flames of fire, and feet like fine brass. As we bow humbly before Him, a great voice will thunder from the heavens, saying:

> *Now the dwelling of God is with men, and he will live with them. They will be his people, and God himself will be with them and be their God. He will wipe every tear from their eyes. There will be no more death or mourning or crying or pain, for the*

old order of things has passed away. (Revelation 21:3-4)

And, again the mighty voice will echo through the corridors of time:

Never again will they hunger; never again will they thirst. The sun will not beat upon them, nor any scorching heat. For the Lamb at the center of the throne will be their shepherd; he will lead them to springs of living water. And God will wipe away every tear from their eyes. (Revelation 7:16-17)

This is the hope of the ages that burns within my breast. It is the ultimate answer to those who suffer and struggle today. It is the only solace for those who have said good-bye to a loved one. Though the pain is indescribable now, we must never forget that our separation is temporary. We will be reunited forever on that glad resurrection morning. As the Scripture promises, our tears will be banished forever!

My father and mother will also be in the crowd on that day, standing expectantly beside my great-grandfather who prayed for me before I was born. They will be straining to catch a glimpse of our arrival, just like they did so many Christmas seasons when we flew into the Kansas City Airport. Dad will have so much to tell me that he will be bursting with excitement. He'll want to take me to some distant planet he's discovered. Your loved ones who died in Christ will also be in that great throng, singing and shouting the praises of the Redeemer. What a celebration it will be!

This is the reward for the faithful—for those who break through the betrayal barrier and persevere to the end. This is the crown of righteousness prepared for those who have fought a good fight, finished the course, and kept the faith (2 Timothy 4:7-8). Throughout our remaining days in this life, therefore, let me urge you not to be discouraged by temporal cares. Accept the circumstances as they are presented to you. Expect periods of hardship to occur, and don't be dismayed when they arrive. "Lean into the pain" when your time to suffer comes around, knowing that God will use the difficulty for His purposes—and, indeed, for our own good. The Lord is very near, and He has promised that your temptation will not be greater than you can bear.

I'll leave you with these wonderful words from Psalm 34:17-19:

> *The righteous cry out, and the Lord hears them; he delivers them from all their troubles. The Lord is close to the brokenhearted and saves those who are crushed in spirit. A righteous man may have many troubles, but the Lord delivers him from them all.*

Whether you received
When God Doesn't Make Sense as a gift,
borrowed it from a friend, or purchased it yourself,
we're glad you read it. Dr. James Dobson, the author
of this book, founded Focus on the Family
in 1977 to address the many challenges and
needs facing today's family.

If this book has been helpful and you would
like to receive more information on child rearing
or other family issues, Focus on the Family
is here to assist you.

www.family.org
(800) A-FAMILY

Because Boys Should Be Boys

bringing up
BOYS

Practical advice and encouragement
for those shaping the next generation of men

DR. JAMES DOBSON

A must-read for every parent from America's most trusted parenting authority.

Also available on audio cassette or CD